ACROSS THE EASTERN ALPS: E5
FROM LAKE CONSTANCE TO VERONA

About the Author

Gillian Price was born in England but moved to Australia when young. After taking a degree in anthropology and working in adult education, she set off to travel through Asia and to trek the Himalayas. The culmination of her journey was Venice, where, her enthusiasm for mountains fired, the next logical step was the Dolomites, only hours away. Starting there, Gillian is steadily exploring the mountain ranges of Italy and bringing them to life for visitors in a series of outstanding guides for Cicerone.

When not out walking with her Venetian husband, or guiding groups, she works as a freelance journalist and screenwriter. An adamant promoter of the use of public transport to minimise impact in Alpine areas, Gillian is an active member of the Italian Alpine Club and the Outdoor Writers' Guild.

Other Cicerone guides by Gillian Price

Walking in the Dolomites
Walking in the Central Italian Alps
Walking in Italy's Gran Paradiso
Walking in Tuscany
Walking in Sicily
Shorter Walks in the Dolomites
Treks in the Dolomites: Alta Via 1 and 2 (co-author)
Walking on Corsica
Trekking in the Apennines – GEA: Grande Escursione Appenninica
Through the Italian Alps – GTA: Grande Traversata delle Alpi

ACROSS THE EASTERN ALPS: E5
FROM LAKE CONSTANCE TO VERONA

by
Gillian Price

2 POLICE SQUARE, MILNTHORPE, CUMBRIA LA7 7PY
www.cicerone.co.uk

A catalogue record for this book is available from the British Library

Maps and diagrams: Nicola Regine
Photos: Gillian Price

Acknowledgements

Along the way I was lucky to have the company of my beloved Nicola, as well as the enthusiastic Story family – Clive, Lucy, Giles and Holly – succeeded by Venetian sisters Marina and Orietta. Thanks to you all!

Gratitude is also due to the Ufficio Idrografico della Provincia di Bolzano, who rushed me a copy of *Clima-Acqua-Valanghe*, their engrossing publication on climate in the Alps. The Provincia di Belluno also helped.

I would also like to acknowledge suggestions from Josef Hubertz, successor in the E5 organisation to Hans Schmidt, who first conceived the route. I trust my work remains true to the original spirit of Hans' idea.

Lastly, a round of applause is in order for the silent team of enthusiasts – including Franco and Helene Cuoghi of Montecchio – who take responsibility for path maintenance and waymarking.

Advice to Readers

Readers are advised that while every effort is taken by the author to ensure the accuracy of this guidebook, changes can occur which may affect its contents. It is advisable to check locally on transport, accommodation, shops, etc., but even rights of way can be altered. The publisher would welcome a note of any such changes.

Front cover: The E5 climbs high above Braunschweiger Hütte and the glacier (Stage 10)

CONTENTS

Introduction 9
Summary of the E5 10
Walking the E5 14
Highlights for Shorter Holidays 16
When to Go 16
Weather 17
To and From the E5 18
Local Transport 19
How to Use this Guidebook 19
Dos and Don'ts 20
Maps 21
What to Take 23
Telephoning 24
Emergencies 24
Currency 26
Accommodation 26
Food and Drink 28
Wildlife 30
Flowers 32
Further Reading 33

Part One Lake Constance to Bozen 35
Stage 1 Constance to Arbon 36
Stage 2 Arbon to Rheineck 40
Stage 3 Rheineck to Lingenau 43
Stage 4 Lingenau to Staufnerhaus 46
Stage 5 Staufnerhaus to Gunzesried 50
Stage 6 Gunzesried to Kemptnerhütte 53
Stage 7 Kemptnerhütte to Memmingerhütte 59
Stage 8 Memmingerhütte to Zams 63
Stage 9 Zams to Mittelberg 67

Stage 10 Mittelberg to Zwieselstein 71
Stage 11 Zwieselstein to Moos in Passeier 76
Stage 12 Moos in Passeier to Pfandleralm 78
Stage 13 Pfandleralm to Hirzerhütte 82
Stage 14 Hirzerhütte to Meranerhütte 85
Stage 15 Meranerhütte to Bozen 90

Part Two Bozen to Verona......................................95
Stage 16 Bozen to Wastlhof 96
Stage 17 Wastlhof to Gfrill 103
Stage 18 Gfrill to Cembra 107
Stage 19 Cembra to Palù di Fersina 110
Stage 20 Palù di Fersina to Levico Terme 115
Stage 21 Levico Terme to Carbonare 122
Stage 22 Carbonare to Passo Coe 126
Stage 23 Passo Coe to Rifugio Lancia 129
Stage 24 Rifugio Lancia to Pian delle Fugazze 134
Stage 25 Pian delle Fugazze to Rifugio Campogrosso 139
Stage 26 Rifugio Campogrosso to Giazza 141
Stage 27 Giazza to Erbezzo 145
Stage 28 Erbezzo to Montecchio 148
Stage 29 Montecchio to Verona 150

APPENDIX 1 Tourist Information 153
APPENDIX 2 German–English Glossary 154
APPENDIX 3 Italian–English Glossary 155

Legend

▬▬▬▬▬ motorway	⌂ accommodation + meals
═══════ sealed road	▥ fort
+++++O+++++ railway, station	† church or shrine
──────── E5 route	◦ town, village
─ ─ ─ ─ walk variant	🚠 cable-car
·············· stretch by public transport	🚌 bus
─·─·─·─ international border	🚂 train
▬▲▬ crest, mountain peak	🛒 groceries
╱╲╱ watercourse	

E5 waymarking

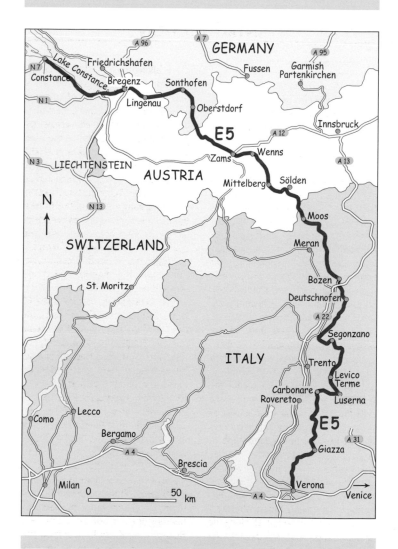

INTRODUCTION

The immensely rewarding and remarkably varied E5 is a recognised European long-distance walking route that makes its way across the Alps from north to south. It starts at Lake Constance in Germany, crosses lowland Switzerland, spends a fair amount of time weaving its way across traditional rural Bavaria and mountainous Austria, before heading due south for Verona in Italy.

The E5 traverses the mighty Alpine chain over a relatively untypical stretch. In contrast to the western Alps, where the overall width is 140km, here in the central section the width bulges out to an impressive 240km, and the route encounters fascinating traditional mountain cultures and languages, and a landscape of soaring snow-capped peaks, immense glaciers, plunging valleys, shimmering lakes, gentle hills with pastureland, then a string of photogenic villages and towns. Probably the only constant factors all along the way are cows and, incidentally, E5 waymarks!

Walking the E5 is both a trek and a journey – an unforgettable one at that – in the footsteps of pilgrims, armies, medieval miners, herdsmen and romantic travellers across the great natural barrier that is the Alps. With a distance of 585.5km (360.7 miles), it takes around a month to complete the 29 stages (which add up to 173 hours). Accumulating 21,000m in height gain and 23,000m in loss, the E5 crosses 26 Alpine passes, drops as low as 59m above sea level and peaks at 2995m. Moreover, it entails five international border crossings, not one of which is manned or requires passport or customs inspection.

An outstanding feature of the E5 is its suitability for walkers of all abilities. While a good part of the route rates as 100% high-altitude Alpine, there are substantial tracts of simpler hill walking. As well as the odd testing climb to deal with, there is also even, level terrain, making for a pace that is decidedly leisurely at times. For example, the first three stages are on mostly flat terrain and can be done in light shoes if preferred.

The E5 was the brainchild of Bavarian walker Hans Schmidt. In 1969 he set off on foot from his home town of Sonthofen, in Germany, heading for his holiday home near Bozen in northern Italy. It took him nine days. A newspaper report of the venture led to a proposal to extend the route in both directions, hence the creation in 1972 of the complete route. However, despite the original plan to further extend the route to the Adriatic coast, and even Venice, this never happened, and today the E5 concludes quite satisfactorily in Verona (though optimistic old signs still refer to it inappropriately as the 'Bodensee–Adria').

SUMMARY OF THE E5

The E5 makes a leisurely start at Constance (Konstanz), following the splendid shores of vast Lake Constance to Bregenz, at the lake's southeastern end. More correctly known as the Bodensee, Lake Constance is Europe's third largest freshwater lake, and Germany's largest. The ancient Romans called it the 'Golden Bowl', the ancient Alemannians the 'Swabian Sea', whereas for Hermann Hesse, who spent an idyllic and fruitful eight years living on its shores, it was 'as far away from Berlin as I can get!'.

Formed by a glacier in a long-gone ice age, Lake Constance lies 400m above sea level. Covering a surface area of 539 sq km (208 sq miles), it extends for 68km (42 miles), the perimeter of its shores adds up to 273km (170 miles) and its waters reach a maximum depth of 252m (827ft). In summer the water temperature is 18–25°C, though this has been known to plummet and the lake to

freeze during exceptionally harsh winters.

Fishing is carried out on a small scale, while the fertile hilly shores support farming and high-standard wine growing. Settlements have dotted the shores of Lake Constance since 6000BC, and intriguing remains of stilt villages can be still seen. The arrival of the Romans and widespread economic development meant the departure of Celtic and Rhaetian peoples, though the area was taken over by the Germanic tribe of the Alemannians after 400AD, when the colonisers had left. Subsequent landmark rulers were the Habsburgs, from 1360.

Lake Constance is both fed and drained by the mighty Rhine River (Rhein), which originates in two separate head streams high in the Swiss Alps. Gathering force as it descends, the Rhine enters the southeastern end of the lake a short distance west of Bregenz, where colossal flood-prevention levees and reinforced parallel riverbeds regulate its flow. Widespread flooding with devastating results is now a thing of the past, thanks to massive works dating back 100 years. The Rhine leaves the lake at Constance and briefly flows west to the Swiss town of Basel, to then head north through Germany's industrial heartland and finally empty into the North Sea, after a total length of 1390km (860 miles).

After Bregenz the E5 goes inland to enter the thickly wooded, undulating, medium-altitude Breganzer Wald.

Remains of ancient pole dwellings on Lake Constance (Stage 1)

Adjacent are the Allgäuer Alps, centring on the Iller river valley. This is the southernmost district of Germany, known as Swabia, and home to a peculiar Bavarian dialect that is utterly incomprehensible to outsiders. The region is characterised by gravel terraces left by long-gone glaciers, and ample fertile terrain that has helped make it the foremost dairy producer in Germany.

This section of the trek is excellent preparation for greater things to come, and come they do, in the shape of Austria's Ötztaler Alps, a region of awe-inspiring white-capped peaks and sprawling glaciers, the result of guaranteed winter snowfalls. The warmth of springtime inevitably causes the snow to melt, and if the meltwater is swollen by rainfall, this creates difficulties for valley communities. Because flood damage was such a problem, flood-data collection first began here in the late 17th century, but according to archive documents, dams and barriers were erected as early as the 1300s, with the purpose of protecting settlements and precious woods from destruction by 'wild mountain torrents'.

Next on the route is a landmark of great interest and key geographical significance – Timmelsjoch, on the Austrian–Italian border, is a major European watershed. On the E5 up until now, the rivers encountered – the Rhine for a start – drained from south to north, ending up in the North Sea. Other significant examples are the Iller and Inn, which head east, joining the Danube on its way to the Black

11

Sea. Timmelsjoch marks a radical change in direction – the watercourses on the Italian side flow south to join the River Adige, which drains into the Adriatic below Venice.

After Timmelsjoch, although the language is still German, and traditional Alpine farming persists, the E5 moves into the South Tyrol, which became part of Italy in the aftermath of the First World War. Very soon after the end of the war the fascists took power in Italy, and in an effort to Italianise the region, Rome gave the inhabitants the agonising choice of either shifting, lock, stock and barrel, to allied neighbouring Austria, or changing their names. Furthermore, 'immigrants' from other parts of Italy were encouraged to 'colonise' the area, and schooling in Italian became compulsory. Curiously enough, today (South Tyrol is now an automous region where 70% are German-speakers) it is the old farming folk, educated under Mussolini's system, who speak better Italian than the young people, who attend segregated German- or Italian-language schools.

Beautiful green valleys characterise the South Tyrol section, then the E5 descends to the historic city of Bozen (marking the end of Part One of the walk as described in this book). This is home to the Ice Man, a Copper Age hunter discovered in a mummified state on a high pass in 1991.

The scenery changes dramatically for the first stage of Part Two, a lengthy 'stroll' parallel to the main Adige river

valley. This river, like the Rhine, has overflowed its banks for centuries, the earliest on record being in 369AD and the latest in 1981. One incident directly involved 16th-century German artist Albrecht Dürer, who was forced to modify his route to Venice.

At slightly lower altitudes the E5 then drops in on a succession of highlights, such as a well-visited sanctuary, then a deep ravine, and the geological wonder Butterloch, all worth looking forward to.

The latter part of the route explores the Trentino region and part of the former Austro-Hungarian Empire. The First World War (also known as the *Guerra Bianca* –'White War' – because it took place in mountainous regions) has left many reminders of the tragic struggles and hardships experienced by troops and locals alike in Trentino. Significant locations on the E5 are the Lagorai mountains, the Folgaria–Lavarone Altopiano and the infamous Pasubio massif.

Strings of imposing wartime constructions, such as forts, are encountered on desolate ridges, as both Austrian and Italian military engineers excelled in this kind of extraordinary building. Lines of barbed wire and trenches still snake their way across landscapes pitted with craters and rubble, the result of incessant mortar fire. Networks of strategic supply tunnels and shelters gouged out of solid rock give an idea of the living

Piccolo Roite with caverns dating back to the First World War (Stage 24)

conditions of the soldiers. Then there are the bare crosses and graves. Nobel prize-winning novelist Ernest Hemingway spent time in 1918 as a volunteer ambulance driver with the American Red Cross on the Pasubio, a landmark experience that inspired him to write the anti-war classic *A Farewell to Arms*. A visit to the Museo Storico Italiano della Guerra (**www.museodellaguerra.it**), housed in a monumental castle at Rovereto, is highly recommended.

The Trentino region also has several curious linguistic pockets. In the 11th century, many Germans migrated south to work in the multitude of mines that were opening up in sparsely populated places across the foothills of the Italian Alps, and in one valley their descendents still speak a version of the original language – Mocheno (see **www.bersntol.it**). Cimbro is also relatively widespread, and there are several explanations for the origin of its name. It could come from the Kimbri people of North Jutland, in Denmark, going all the way back to 200AD, although the more widely accepted version relates to lower Bavaria. Lumberjacks and woodsmen were known as *Zimberer* (similar to the modern German *Zimmerman* for 'carpenter'), hence Zimbri, Cimbri.

The E5's final southern leg passes through thriving farming communities in the rolling Monti Lessini. Because of its wealth of extraordinary fossils, a legacy of its ancient marine past, Monti Lessini is a protected *parco regionale* (**www.lessiniapark.it**).

The trek finally wanders through vineyards to conclude in beautiful Verona, romantic city par excellence.

WALKING THE E5

The variety along the route of the E5 is extraordinary. A day spent strolling along a valley floor conversing with cows can be followed by one clambering alongside an awe-inspiring glacier or exploring an old Alpine sanctuary. On occasions the E5 makes use of public transport, in the shape of buses and cable-cars, in order to avoid uninteresting stretches of asphalt, and these are a pleasant rest for the weary.

In this book the route has been divided into two parts, corresponding to approximately a fortnight in each case.

Part One (Stages 1–15) starts out at Lake Constance and crosses Germany's Allgäuer Alps and Austria's Ötztaler Alps, concluding at Bozen in Italy.

Part Two (Stages 16–29) leaves Bozen parallel to the Adige river valley. The Lagorai and Pasubio groups of mountains are traversed, before a gentle descent via the Monti Lessini to Verona.

To avoid confusion, this guidebook keeps to the original stage-per-day divisions of the E5, but as this can mean a maximum of nine hours and minimum of two hours per day, suggestions for splitting or extending such stages are given in the route description. Every stage concludes at either a village or Alpine hut where

both accommodation (be it dormitory or hotel style), meals (dinner and breakfast) and a hot shower are available. Shops for stocking up on groceries are found in most settlements, as is public transport, which allows you to personalise the route and slot in or out as you please, or in line with changing weather conditions.

Waymarking

Waymarking varies considerably along the E5. 'E5' appears regularly on maps, but much less so on the ground, and a compass is often a great help. On the initial section, along the shores of Lake Constance, a string of local footpaths, such as the Thurgauer Rundwanderweg, is used. Also, the first half of the E5 runs through German-speaking regions, and *Fernwanderweg* means 'long-distance pathway', so in places the E5 is signed 'EFW5'. Once the E5 crosses into Italy, however, waymarks are exclusively red/white in accordance with Alpine Club usage.

For the most part good paths are used and no special mountaineering expertise is necessary. The main requisites are a decent level of fitness, curiosity about Alpine cultures and geography, common sense, and determination to get up those steep paths.

Generally speaking it is inadvisable to attempt the E5 in the opposite direction to the original north–south plan, as waymarking is rarely bi-directional and it is easy to lose your sense of direction.

Signpost on the E5

● **Kemptner-Hütte** ☒ ⊡ **2 h** 438
● **Grosser Krottenkopf** 2 ½ h 432/438
DAV Sektion Allgäu Kempten

1 h 439

● Schochenalptal ☒ ⊡ 5 h 439/432
● Rappensee-Hütte 4 h 439
● Steinscharte
DAV Sektion Allgäu Kempten

1 h 438

● Holzgau (E5)
DAV Sektion Allgäu Kempten

Rossgumpenalpe ☒
Ober-Lechtal Tourismus

Rossgumpenalpe ☒ **5 min**
Ober Lechtal Tourismus

Via Alpina

HIGHLIGHTS FOR SHORTER HOLIDAYS

Not everyone has 29 days to dedicate to a trek such as this, but excellent public transport links make it feasible to slot in at convenient points and enjoy the best parts of the route, according to individual holiday limits.

It is also worth noting that the majority of German walkers doing the E5 join the route at Oberstdorf on Stage 6, thus skipping the 'tame' stages along Lake Constance and across the Vorarlberg. What's more, many head home from Bozen, having completed the 'Alpine' segment which is Part One. The result is that Part Two, the southern section towards Verona, is much quieter.

The following are suggestions for shorter holidays.

- **5 Days** From Oberstdorf (Stage 6) in the Bavarian Alps, approaching the Ötztaler Alps for a traverse in a truly glacial setting, exiting at Zwieselstein near Sölden (Stage 10). This is the Alpine heart of the E5, with dramatic landscapes.
- **4 Days** From Moos in Passeier (Stage 12), passing through typical South Tyrol pastoral scenery alternating with rugged mountains, to the historic town of Bozen (Stage 15).
- **5 Days** Setting out from Bozen (Stage 16) on a dizzy cable-car, this entails a long traverse punctuated by fascinating geological

and historic landmarks, before a climb over the wild Lagorai range, descending on the resort town of Levico Terme in Valsugana (Stage 20).

- **5 Days** Carbonare (Stage 22) is the launching point for a stunning section across the Pasubio and Carega mountains, ending in the quiet village of Giazza (Stage 26).

WHEN TO GO

As this is a predominantly Alpine route, it is suitable for the summer months, when snow on the high passes will have either melted or be soft and manageable. However, another factor that must be taken into account for holiday planning is accommodation, and the periods when high-altitude huts, as well as hotels lower down, are open. The huts are mostly open and manned from late June through to late September, though walkers planning around the start or end of the season should check in advance, as bad weather may affect these times. This rule also applies to family-run guesthouses and bed and breakfasts in small villages. Opening times for accommodation are included in the route description. Having said that, lower altitude stretches, e.g. below the 1000m mark, such as Lake Constance and the Lessini, along with many intermediate sections, can be followed pleasurably year round.

Inspiring views from Hirzerhütte (Stage 13)

WEATHER

*'If the rooster crows from the dung
heap the weather will either
change or stay the same.'*
Age-old wisdom from Alpine farmers

Walkers who do not have easy access to poultry farms are advised to consult up-to-date weather forecasts, which are posted daily in most tourist offices and mountain huts. If in doubt, enquire locally. Additionally, an altimeter can double as a barometer. When the altitude reading for a known place such as a hut goes up for no apparent reason, then the atmospheric pressure has dropped and the weather may change for the worse. On the other hand, when an altitude reading drops, the pressure has risen and good weather is probable. (It is good practice to calibrate your altimeter each day.)

Walking in the Alps in summertime typically embraces a huge range of weather. Blazing sun, perfect blue skies and light breezes tend to be the norm, but there may also be long periods of persistent rain and storms, and even snow. When conditions appear unsuitable for walking, never hesitate to change your plans. It's definitely preferable to 'waste' a day or two (resting? investigating cultural aspects of the area?) than to end up on the front page of the newspaper, 'star' of a mountain accident or helicopter rescue. Where possible, several straightforward escape routes are given in the route description.

17

TO AND FROM THE E5

The official starting point of the E5 is at the German town of Constance on the southern shore of the Bodensee (Lake Constance), and well served by trains and buses. The route's conclusion, at the romantic Italian city of Verona, lies on the upper edge of northern Italy's Po plain, with access to major transport networks. (See Overview Map, page 8.)

Air

The closest airports are:

- Friedrichshafen **www.fly-away.de** (Ryanair from the UK) is 25km away, on the northern shore of Lake Constance. Allow 1 hour by car or bus and ferry to reach Constance.
- Zurich **www.zurich-airport.com** (British Airways), 75km away in neighbouring Switzerland, is conveniently linked by a 1-hour train ride to Constance.
- Verona's Valerio Catullo Airport **www.aeroportoverona.it** (British Airways) is served by frequent buses to the nearby city.
- Brescia's Gabriele D'Annunzio airport **www.aeroportoverona.it** (Ryan Air) is linked by bus to both the town of Brescia and to Verona.
- Bozen's small airport has mostly domestic flights, but also many special summer charters **www.abd-airport.it**.

Rail

Constance is easily reached by direct trains from Germany (timetable

St Leonhard (Stage 12)

information at **www.bahn.de**) and Switzerland (**www.sbb.ch/pv**) as well as from Bregenz in Austria (**www.oebb.at**). Italian rail services for the later sections of the E5 – principally Bozen, Levico Terme and Verona – can be consulted at **www.trenitalia.it**.

Water
A fleet of photogenic ferries regularly plies Lake Constance, with extra services in summer. Included is a useful car ferry from Friedrichshafen to Romanshorn. Timetable and route information can be obtained from the relevant tourist offices (see Appendix 1).

Kohlern cable-car (Stage 16)

LOCAL TRANSPORT

ÖBB-Postbus at **www.postbus.at** for all bus services in Austria (e.g. Bregenz to Lingenau in the Vorarlberg region, Wenns to Mittelberg in Tirol).

SAD ☎ (39) 800/846047 (toll-free) or **www.sad.it** for long-distance public transport throughout Italy's South Tyrol/Alto Adige region. Exceptions are local buses, along with the Jenesien/San Genesio and Kohlern/Colle cable-cars, which come under ☎ (39) 0471/978545 **www.sasabz.it**.

Trentino Trasporti ☎ (39) 0461/821000 **www.ttspa.it** covers the Trentino region and extends to Pian delle Fugazze.

Ferrovie Tramvie Vicentine ☎ (39) 0444/223115 **www.ftv.vi.it** does the summertime runs from Pian delle

Fugazze and Rifugio Campogrosso down to Vicenza.

Verona APTV ☎ (39) 045/8057911 **www.apt.vr.it** serves the Monti Lessini villages of Giazza and Erbezzo.

Verona AMT ☎ (39) 045/8871111 **www.amt.it** for local Verona buses, namely Avesa to the city centre.

HOW TO USE THIS GUIDEBOOK

The route is divided into Parts One and Two, as well as day stages. Each stage has an information box covering the following.

Time The actual walking time is given, as well as a separate figure for bus and cable-car trips. A couple of extra hours should always be allowed for rest stops, detours and non-scheduled activities.

Distance Given in both kilometres and miles, but excluding stretches covered by bus or cable-car.

Ascent/Descent Given in metres. This means how much the route climbs and drops in total during that stage. With the exception of the first three stages, this is a much more important indicator of the strenuousness of the day's walking than is distance.

Grade Given on a scale of 1–3; an indicator of the difficulty involved in that day, as follows.

- Grade 1 is a straightforward path with a moderate incline, *suitable for all ranges of walkers*.
- Grade 2 refers to a *fairly strenuous section of Alpine walking*, but without any special difficulties.
- Grade 3 requires some experience on Alpine terrain, as *some stretches may be exposed or unduly difficult*. A head for heights is helpful, along with orientation skills.

During the route description, 'road' means the way is surfaced, while 'track' or 'lane' means unsurfaced. 'Path' always refers to a pedestrians-only way.

Compass bearings are given (N, SW, NNW and so forth), as is right (R) and left (L). Useful landmarks appear in **bold** type, with their altitude in metres (100m = 328ft), abbreviated as 'm', and not to be confused with 'min' for minutes.

DOS AND DON'TS

- *Do* prepare properly for the trek. Be as fit as possible, as this will maximise your enjoyment. Exhaustion does not enhance Alpine landscapes, and more importantly, a healthy walker reacts better in an emergency.
- *Don't* overload your rucksack. Submit it to the bathroom scales – 10kg is a reasonable cut-off point. (Shampoo and creams can be transferred to smaller containers, for example.) Remember, too, that you'll have the extra weight of food and water each day. Be strict and leave any non-essentials (such as the paperback you're in the middle of) at home. (See also, What to Take.)
- *Do* start out early each morning. Generally speaking, bad weather and storms roll in during the afternoon. Further, it's essential to allow extra

time for rest stops, wrong turns, missing signposts, and detours due to collapsed bridges, for example.

- *Don't* walk on your own and *do* stick with your companions – there's safety in numbers.
- *Do* be honest with yourself and *don't* be overly ambitious. Plan stages to suit your capabilities and read the route description before setting out.
- *Do* check weather forecasts, and if necessary modify your day's walking accordingly. Adverse weather conditions can transform even a Grade 1 path into a perilous enterprise. In the unlikely event that you are caught out in a storm, avoid metallic fixtures and rid yourself of all metallic objects. It is *not* advisable to take shelter under rock overhangs and isolated trees. Recommended techniques include curling up into a ball or lying flat on the ground.
- *Do* leave word of your intended walking route; sign the register in mountain huts and include the following day's destination.
- *Don't* leave common sense at home; take all your rubbish away with you, and be considerate when making a toilet stop.

MAPS

Simplified sketch maps and route profiles detailing each stage are included in this guide. Their purpose is to give a rough idea of the route, and to describe facilities walkers can expect to find. However, it is essential to take with you the relevant published maps.

Kompass (**www.kompass.at**) publish two useful maps covering the whole of the E5. 'Wanderkarte Europäischer Fernwanderweg E5' sheet 120 is 'Teil Nord' (northern part), which corresponds to Stages 1–9, while sheet 121 'Teil Süd' covers Stages 10–29. At a 1:50,000 scale, they consist of strip sections of larger maps, and in combination with this guide are perfectly adequate for following the E5. Their disadvantages

are occasional innaccuracies and lack of detail, and the fact that they only show the immediate area around the route; it can be frustrating not being able to identify more distant mountains.

Walkers who intend to cover a short part of the route may prefer purchasing more detailed maps. Apart from Kompass, other possibilities are listed below, though there are some gaps. Leading map sellers and outdoor stores in the UK, USA and Australia generally keep these in stock. For the UK try Stanfords (**www.stanfords.co.uk**).

Stages 1–3 1:60,000 sheet Bodensee/ Lake Constance by Kummerly+ Frey (Constance to Bregenz) **www.swissmaps.ch**.

Checking the map near Rossgumpenalm (Stage 7)

Stages 6–7 Alpenvereinskarte 1:25,000 sheet 2/1 Allgäuer-Lechtaler Alpen, West (Oberstdorf to Holzgau only). Published by the Austrian Alpine Club; members can order the map at **www.alpenverein.at/karten**.

Stages 7–8 Alpenvereinskarte 1:25,000 sheet 3/3 Lechtaler Alpen, Parseierspitze (Holzgau to Zams only). Published by the Austrian Alpine Club; members can order the map at **www.alpenverein.at/karten**.

Stage 10 Alpenvereinskarte 1:25,000 sheet 30/5 Ötztaler Alpen, Geigenkamm (Mittelberg to Zwieselstein). Published by the Austrian Alpine Club; members can order the map at **www.alpenverein.at/karten**.

Stages 11–13 Tabacco 1:25,000 sheet 039 'Val Passiria/Passeiertal' (Zwieselstein to Hirzerhütte).

Stage 14 Tabacco 1:25,000 sheet 011 'Merano e dintorni/Meran und Umgebung' (Hirzerhütte to Meranerhütte).

Stage 15–16 Tabacco 1:25,000 sheet 034 'Bolzano-Renon-Tschögglberg' (St Jakob to Deutschnofen only).

Stage 16 Tabacco 1:25,000 sheet 029 'Sciliar/Schlern' (Bozen to Oberraden).

Stages 23–24 Sezioni Vicentine del CAI 1:25,000 sheet 2 (*foglio nord*) 'Sentieri Pasubio Carega' (Passo Coe to Pian delle Fugazze).

Stages 25–27 Sezioni Vicentine del CAI 1:25,000 sheet 1 (*foglio sud*) 'Sentieri Pasubio Carega' (Pian delle Fugazze to Maregge only).

Stage 29 Provincia di Verona-Comune di Verona 1:20,000 'Carta dei Sentieri Sulle Colline di Verona' (Montecchio to Verona).

A brief note on names. The German language often uses 'ß' instead of 'ss'. One common instance is 'Straße' (road), pronounced 'strasse' not 'strabe'. Having said that, visitors will find numerous examples of simplification to 'ss' on signs and maps. In the Italian South Tyrol, where place names exist in both German and Italian (though this is often simply a historic translation found on maps and never actually used by the people), in the route description both are given at the first occurrence, and subsequently the former only.

WHAT TO TAKE

Inappropriate gear can turn an enjoyable walking holiday into a nightmare, so it's worth spending time beforehand on careful preparation. The following is a checklist with suggestions.

- Comfortable lightweight rucksack, preferably no heavier than 10kg when packed. Plastic bags or stuff bags for organising contents.
- Sturdy walking boots with good grip and ankle support (not brand new). Sandals or trainers for the evening.
- Lightweight sleeping sheet (sleeping bag liner), essential for stays in mountain huts.
- Small towel, personal toiletries.
- Basic first aid kit and essential medicines.
- Waterproofs. Depending on personal taste, either a full poncho that covers your rucksack, or a jacket, over-trousers and rucksack cover. (A lightweight folding umbrella may be appreciated by walkers who wear glasses.)
- Telescopic trekking poles – to ease rucksack weight, aid wonky knees, boost confidence during steep descents and stream crossings, keep sheep dogs at a safe distance, hang out washing...
- Sun hat, shades, lip salve and extra-high-factor sunblock (the sun's UV rays become stronger by 10% for every 1000m in ascent).
- Layered clothing to cope with conditions ranging from biting cold winds through to scorching sun, e.g. T-shirts, short and long trousers (jeans are definitely not suitable), warm fleece and a windproof jacket, as well as a woolly hat and gloves.
- Water bottle – plastic mineral-water bottles are perfect.

- Emergency food, e.g. muesli bars, biscuits and chocolate.
- Walking maps and compass.
- Whistle, and torch or headlamp (with spare batteries), for calling for help (as well as exploring wartime tunnels).
- Altimeter, binoculars, and camera with either plenty of film, or battery recharger with adaptor and memory cards.
- Gaiters for snow traverses.
- Supply of euros in cash, and credit card (ATMs are listed in the route description).
- Salt tablets or electrolyte powders – to combat depletion due to sweating, and to prevent dehydration.
- Pegs or safety pins for drying washing on rucksack.

TELEPHONING

The route crosses four European countries, but little changes in terms of telephones. If calling from overseas the individual country code is needed: 41 for Switzerland, 44 for Germany, 43 for Austria and 39 for Italy. Once inside the country, dial a number without the initial zero – the exception to this is Italy, where the full area code is essential at all times, apart from toll-free calls starting with 800 and calls to mobile phones that begin with the number 3. (In German a mobile phone is *Handy* and in Italian *cellulare*.)

Public telephones requiring a prepaid card or coins are plentiful. There is generally decent mobile phone reception in towns and villages. In mountain valleys, passes and most high-altitude huts the signal is often weak, if not completely absent. Overseas visitors are generally at an advantage, however, as their phones

usually have access to the full range of private networks. **Remember your phone charger and an adaptor**.

EMERGENCIES

'Help' is *Zu Hilfe* in German and *aiuto* (pronounced 'eye-yoo-toh') in Italian.

The Europe-wide emergency phone number is 112. This will get you through to the nearest emergency service, and like the numbers listed below, it can be dialled from a mobile phone – even if you're out of credit.

Individual country telephone numbers for alerting emergency services are as follows.

Austria: *Gendarmerie* (police) ☎ 133; *Bergrettung* (mountain rescue) ☎ 140

Germany: *Polizei* (police) ☎ 110; *Rettung* (rescue) ☎112

Italy: *polizia* (police) ☎ 113; *ambulanza, soccorso alpino* (ambulance, mountain rescue) ☎ 118

Switzerland: *Polizei* **(police)** ☎ 117; *Sanitätsnotruf* (health emergencies) ☎ 144

Old-fashioned audible or visible signals have not gone out of style, and walkers are advised to commit to memory the following simple procedures. Using either a whistle, or a lamp (torch) after dark, the internationally recognised call for help is **six** signals per minute, to be repeated after a minute's pause. The answer is **three** signals per minute, to be repeated after a minute's pause. Anyone who hears a call for help must contact the nearest police station or refuge as quickly as possible.

When talking to the emergency services be prepared to provide as much of the following information as possible: your name, where you are (landmarks, altitude), the nature of the accident, how many people need help with what type of injuries, atmospheric conditions, any obstacles for a helicopter (e.g. overhead cables).

Residents in countries belonging to the European Union should be in possession of a European Health Insurance Card (EHIC). As of January 2006 this replaces the E111 and entitles the holder to free or reduced-cost reciprocal health treatment in all the countries covered by this guide, Switzerland included. Applications by UK residents can be made online at **www.dh.gov.uk** ('Policy and Guidance' section). Forms are also available at post offices, along with a 'Health Advice for Travellers' leaflet.

However, travel insurance to cover a walking holiday is also

The following arm signals could be useful for communicating at a distance or with a helicopter:

Both arms raised
- Help needed
- Land here
- YES (to pilot's questions)

One arm raised diagonally, one arm down diagonally
- Help not needed
- Do not land here
- NO (to pilot's questions)

Other useful devices to aid a helicopter pilot are:
- coloured clothes laid on the ground (well-anchored)
- smoke signals
- SOS (preferably in two-metre high letters) written in the snow, by using footprints or stones, can also be useful.

strongly recommended – and is *essential* for non-Europeans. Members of Alpine Clubs generally have such insurance, which covers helicopter rescue, which otherwise can be extremely costly. In Britain walkers can apply to the British Mountaineering Council **www.thebmc.co.uk** ☎ 0870 0104878 or the UK branch of the Austrian Alpine Club **www.aacuk.uk.com** ☎ 01707 386740.

CURRENCY

Luckily the euro is used throughout Germany, Austria and Italy, although Switzerland still has Swiss Francs (approximately SFr1.50 = 1 euro at the time of writing). Euro bank notes are normally accepted in Switzerland, though change will usually be given in local currency. Credit cards are a good idea in towns (hotels, restaurants, railway ticket offices), though they are of no help at all in mountain huts or bed and breakfasts, so always carry a good supply of euros. (All the sizeable towns visited by the route have ATMs.)

ACCOMMODATION

Guesthouses in small villages are an important source of accommodation along the E5. On the northern sections this means excellent value bed and breakfasts in spotless private homes, starting at around 20 euros per person (at the time of writing). In Italy accommodation tends to be marginally pricier, and half-board (with dinner

Sign for accommodation on the E5

and breakfast included) is often the rule in summer. A few youth hostels (*Jugendherberge*) are also listed: **www.jugendherberge.de** for those in Germany, **www.youthhostel.ch** in Switzerland and **www.jgh.at** for Austria.

The invariably helpful tourist offices in small towns en route can usually find accommodation at the last minute.

The E5 also uses a number of brilliantly positioned mountain huts. Akin to hostels, and known as *Hütte* in German and *rifugio* in Italian, the majority are run by national Alpine clubs – ŒAV (Oesterreichischer Alpenverein) **www.alpenverein.at** is the Austrian club, DAV (Deutscher Alpenverein) the German sister **www.alpenverein.de**, AVS (Alpenverein Südtirol) **www.alpenverein.it** belongs to the South Tyrol, SAT (Società Alpinistica Trentino) **www.sat.tn.it** covers the Trentino region of Italy, while CAI (Club Alpino Italiano) **www.cai.it** is the broad-based Italian association. All have discounted rates for their own members, as well as for those belonging to similar clubs with reciprocal agreements. British walkers can join the UK branch of the Austrian Alpine Club **www.aacuk.uk.com** ☎ 01707 386740, or the British Mountaineering Council **www.thebmc.co.uk** ☎ 0870 0104878.

In general advance booking is not necessary for huts in Austria and

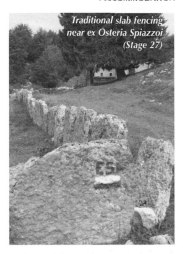

Traditional slab fencing near ex Osteria Spiazzoi (Stage 27)

Germany, as the policy is to have 50% of total beds available each day for new arrivals, and no one is turned away. Walkers planning on weekends in August – peak holiday time – may prefer to book ahead, as should large groups. Reservations should be made by fax (or e-mail) and a deposit sent. (Hardly any huts have a direct phone line – see individual hut listings in the route description.)

The situation is different in Italy, however, where it is advisable to phone (direct line) and book, as the huts are much smaller and the staff prefer to know how many people to expect for meals. One day ahead is usually sufficient in non-peak periods.

Sleeping accommodation is either in rooms (*Zimmer* in German, *camera* in Italian) or dormitories (*Lager/dormitorio*), with charges per person starting

27

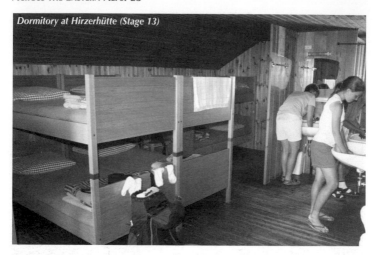
Dormitory at Hirzerhütte (Stage 13)

at around 8 euros. A personal sheet sleeping bag or bag liner (*Schlafsack/sacco lenzuola*) is compulsory, and a small towel is essential for those intent on enjoying a timed hot shower (*Dusche/doccia*), for which a token (extra charge) is usually needed. Bathrooms are always shared, and queues can form. The German and Austrian huts also provide a special room for drying gear (*Trockenraum*). All huts have a place to leave boots (*Schuhraum*) as only light footwear may be worn inside.

A few general hut rules are worth noting.
- Service usually stops between 10pm and 6am, which may also be the 'lights out' period, as the generator will be turned off where relevant.

- Payment is almost exclusively accepted in cash only, so go prepared. It's a good idea to settle bills in the evening to streamline your morning departure.
- Meals are generally at set times, and these differ wildly from establishment to establishment. (Watch out for early kitchen closing in the German-speaking huts!)

FOOD AND DRINK

In German-speaking countries *Frühstuck* (breakfast) unfailingly means *Brot* (bread) with butter and jam, *Käse* (cheese) and *Schinken* (ham), a choice of *Kaffee* (coffee), *Tee* (tea) or *Kakao* (hot chocolate). Sometimes there are even *Eier* (boiled eggs), muesli and yoghurt.

Al fresco dining at Memmingerhütte (Stage 7)

Abendessen (dinner) at a local restaurant or mountain hut will be a generous serving of meat, be that *Schwein* (pork), *Rind* (beef) or *Kalb* (veal), with a *Beilage* (side serving) of *Kartoffeln* (potatoes), then *gemischte Salat* (mixed salad) or other *Gemüse* (vegetables). Vegetarians can usually request an omelette.

In Italy *colazione* (breakfast) is a lighter affair: *pane* (bread) with *burro* (butter) and *marmellata* (jam), accompanied by coffee, usually with milk as *caffelatte*, and *tè* or *cioccolata calda*.

Cena (dinner) starts with a *primo* (first course), which will be a substantial pasta dish in most cases, though many huts serve soups such as *minestrone* with vegetables. The *primo* will be followed by a *secondo* of meat, probably *manzo* (beef), *maiale* (pork), *vitello* (veal) or *pollo* (chicken), then a *contorno* (side dish) of *verdura* (vegetables) or *insalata* (salad).

Regional specialties en route include delicate whitefish or eel from Lake Constance, and the Vorarlberg region of Austria offers *Kässpätzle* – home-made noodles baked with melted cheese and accompanied by potato salad. One widely enjoyed dessert is *hausgemacht Apfelstrudel* (homemade apple strudel), which usually comes with *Sahne* (cream), *Eis* (ice cream) or *Vanillasös* (vanilla sauce). An unusual dish from Italy's South Tyrol is *Strauben* – squiggles of sweet, fried batter served with jam.

Drinks include well-chilled *Bier*, usually *vom Fass* (on tap), as well as combinations such as *Radler*, a variation of shandy but with lemon soda. *Holundersaft* is a fragrant cordial of elderberry blossom. Be wary of *schnapps*, a clear but near-lethal spirit often distilled from pears.

Wine lovers have a lot to look forward to on the E5. The list opens at Lake Constance, with a fruity white made from the Müller-Thurgau grapes grown on the hills overlooking the lake's sun-blessed southern shores. There's also an unusual rosé with a golden sheen, known as Weissherbst.

The Italian South Tyrol has plenty of surprises in store on the wine front. The Bozen basin acts as a sun trap, and encourages the cultivation of grapes for some superb reds, Lagrein and Blauburgunder (also known as pinot nero) for a start, while the mild climate of nearby Lago di Caldaro results in a light Kalderersee table wine. A divine amber dessert wine is the aromatic Gewurztraminer, which originated in the Termin district nearby. Moving south, a 'must taste' is the full-bodied Teroldego from the Trentino region. At walk's end you'll be spoiled for choice, as the Verona district has reds – Valpolicella and the amazing Amarone – or the white Soave.

WILDLIFE

Nimble **chamois** (mountain goats) can often be observed grazing on Alpine mountainsides, close to the snowline. Dainty, and amazingly fleet of foot on

Marmots

near-vertical cliffs, they sport short, crochet-hook horns and characteristic black-and-cream striped faces. Herds comprise mainly females and young, while the males keep their distance, often crying mournfully at passers-by. Sharing high-altitude pasture, but much less common and considerably heftier, is the **ibex** (or steinbok). These stocky creatures have imposing ridged horns in the males, and somewhat shorter horns for the females. The mixed herds include young males who challenge each other to mock fights, clashing horns while tottering upright on their back legs.

One memorable Alpine resident is the **marmot**, said to resemble a prairie dog or beaver, though its name comes from the Latin for 'mountain mouse'. Chubby, playful, furry herbivores, marmots spend their summers on medium-altitude pasture slopes above 1200m, on an earnest quest for tasty flowers and tender grass. A lookout watches over the group, and an ear-piercing alarm whistle signals danger from birds of prey or foxes, for example, and brings all the members rushing back to the protection of the communal den. Snuggling deep in their roomy burrows, marmots go into hibernation from around October to March.

In medium-altitude mountainous zones the jet-black **salamander** comes out after rain, its glossy, almost prehistoric body waddling clumsily. A rare treat at lower altitudes, usually amongst trees, is the **fire salamander**, a legendary creature long attributed with natural immunity to flames.

Birds of prey are a fairly constant sight along the E5, beginning at Lake Constance where the **peregrine falcon** is commonly seen. The lake's plentiful fish stocks (notably perch and white-fish) also guarantee a flourishing

31

waterfowl population – **cormorants**, **swans**, **moorhens**, **coots** and **herons**, to name but a few. Reeds line the shore in many places, encouraging nesting conditions. **Storks** have also been sighted regularly on the southern shore (see Stage 1).

A string of nature reserves lines the lake, notably the 2000-hectare Rhine Delta, with a record 330 bird species in wetland, riparian forest and reedy marshes.

The best method for spotting birds of prey is to glance skywards from time to time, as they usually glide, surveying pasture and clearings. Also, keep listening for their distinctive cries – the **buzzard** for instance emits a mewing 'peeeeoo'.

The only potentially dangerous animal is the **viper**, a light-grey snake with distinctive diamond markings on its back. It only usually attacks humans when threatened, so if encountered on the path, give it time to slither away. A bite is rarely fatal, though not to be under-rated, and medical assistance is imperative. While awaiting help, the victim should be kept calm and still, and the affected limb bandaged to restrict circulation.

FLOWERS

Wonderful experiences are guaranteed for even the least attentive flower observer. Intensely scented **black vanilla orchids** are one of the delights of high-altitude meadows. Their tiny pyramidal heads, of a

High-altitude violets

deep, red-brown hue, peek through the grass, and to appreciate their concentrated chocolate fragrance it is necessary to smell them close up (cows that eat them are said to produce chocolate-flavoured milk!). Divinely blue **gentians** are common, while the legendary, creamy coloured, felty **edelweiss** is a rarer sight these days. Open grassy mountainsides may

Creeping avens grows on scree

Tunnel on the Strada degli Eroi (Stage 24)

feature the curious **carline thistle**, an inspiration for watercolour artists. Its spiky, tentacle leaves reach out from a central cluster, and the sizable, creamy coloured cardboard-like flowers have the habit of closing up tightly into a ball in the damp. According to mountain lore they are good forecasters – when closed, a sign of bad weather, and vice versa.

FURTHER READING

Italian Journey 1786–1788, Johann Wolfgang von Goethe, Princeton University Press (1989)

Clima-Acqua-Valanghe, Ufficio Idrografico della Provincia di Bolzano (2002)

Alpine Flowers of Britain and Europe, C Grey-Wilson and M Blamey, HarperCollins (1995)

33

Waterfalls opposite Kemptnerhütte (Stage 6)

PART ONE
Lake Constance to Bozen (15 days)

The colossal E5 route begins in a leisurely manner. From Constance it follows the beautiful southern shores of Lake Constance, crossing borders from Germany to Switzerland and Austria. It then proceeds over a minor crest belonging to the Allgäuer Alps, before dipping across the strategic Iller valley to the transport hub of Oberstdorf in German Bavaria. At this point walkers have their first taste of the 'real' Alps, and there are several overnight stays in well-run mountain huts amidst magnificent scenery. A mammoth stage flanking (without actually crossing) awesome glaciers in the Austrian Ötztal is a memorable highlight. The E5 then ventures into Italy by way of traditional high-altitude hamlets, dropping to the charming town of Bozen, where the backdrop comprises the monumental Dolomites. This marks the conclusion of the E5's captivating northern Alpine section. This substantial opening section covers a fascinating array of landscapes and cultures. Walkers can rest assured that boredom will not be an issue!

The historic university town of Constance (Konstanz) occupies a pretty spot in the far southern reaches of Germany. It stands on a strategic corner of Lake Constance where the River Rhine begins its course to the North Sea. The delightful medieval core of Constance has attractively decorated buildings and even, surprisingly, replicas of five great basilicas in Rome, thanks to zealous 10th-century bishops.

On the harbourside is a remarkable ancient grain store, which hosted the landmark 1414–18 Church Council of Constance, the Konzil Gaststätten. The many outcomes of the council included: reuniting the Catholic church by reducing the popes from three to one; condemning the Protestant teachings of John Wycliffe; and burning at the stake 'heretic' reformer Jan Hus.

Visitors clad in walking gear are not new to the town, as it was a key point for pilgrims in medieval times, and served as a stopover for those heading for Rome, Santiago di Compostela and even Jerusalem.

Accommodation at English-speaking Susan's Guestroom ☎ (49) 07531/45915 **www.susans-guestroom.com** or bed and breakfast at Turm Café ☎ (49) 07531/22228, otherwise there's a decent pick of hotels and a youth hostel ☎ (49) 07531/32260. ⓘ (49) 07531/133030.

STAGE 1
Constance to Arbon

Time	6hr 30min
Distance	27.6km/17.1 miles
Ascent/Descent	Negligible
Grade	1

The first stage, along the shores of Lake Constance, is a great introduction to this huge body of fresh water, with its abundance of fish, waterfowl and peregrine falcons. For the most part clear pathways are followed over flat terrain – through restful woodland and cultivated farmland, punctuated by rambling homesteads in traditional design. There are some stretches of asphalted road as the E5 ducks in and out of lakeside villages, but traffic is light, and at most may mean leisurely cyclists. A string of pretty picnic and swimming spots is encountered, not mention inviting places to eat, so lunch can be taken in various ways.

This is rather a long day, but easily shortened by staying at a hotel en route, or taking a ferry or train. A helpful string of stations is never far from the lakefront, and the automatic ticket machines accept euros and credit cards as well as Swiss francs.

Note There is no official E5 waymarking until Stage 4, though orientation is not a problem, as other signed routes are used. Outside the villages landmarks can be confusing, as there are multiple Seedorfs (lake hamlets) and 'Am Schiff' (boat) guesthouses.

Depart **Constance** (395m) in a southeasterly direction from the ferry harbour and adjacent railway station on the waterfront, following signposts for the Bodensee Wanderweg. Follow the train line past the Sea Life Aquarium, and out of Germany via a customs checkpoint. Now in Switzerland, proceed along Seestraße to the modest marina of **Kreuzlingen** ⓘ (41) 0171/672384.

Next to the tourist office the yellow Wanderweg signs point you through lovely Seeburgpark, full of squirrels, past animal pens, snack bars and the See Museum, and close to the attractive Hörnliberg youth hostel ☎ (41) 071/6882663. Another marina is crossed and a lakefront promenade joined, with a camping ground and places to eat.

Some 20min along the promenade you emerge at office buildings. Cross the road and dog-leg R to continue along the path. Soon, in common with a surfaced cycle track, you pass **Bottighofen** railway station and continue alongside the train line for 15min, before crossing the grounds of Münsterlingen Psychiatric Hospital. A pretty path follows, hugging the water's edge, to reach a cosy hamlet named Seedorf, where there are more restaurants. Birdwatchers will be interested to know that for several years storks have been nesting along the Zollershus-Güttingen stretch that follows.

The next useful reference point is classy Restaurant Schiff at (just for a change...) Seedorf, aka **Kesswil**. Offshore, the poles sticking up out of the water are the remains of ancient stilt dwellings, and modern-day fishing huts jut out from the shore as well. Once through the village of **Uttwil** (Hotel Bad Uttwil ☎ (41) 071/46344 84) you're on a quiet road flanking the railway track en route to the popular Holzenstein baths and a huge swimming pool complex. The lakefront path resumes through immaculately kept public gardens and around the corner S to

4hr 15min – Romanshorn (399m). Formerly a fishing village, these days

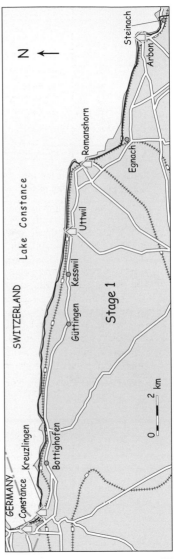

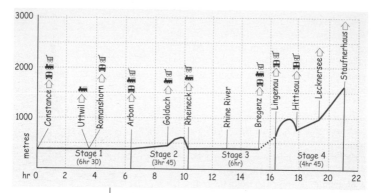

Romanshorn is a bustling harbour town. ⓘ (41) 071/4633232. Youth hostel ☎ (41) 071/4631717, Hotel Schloss ☎ (41) 071/4667800 **www.hotelschloss.ch**. Shops, ATM, trains and ferries for Arbon.

Lake Constance, early morning

From the harbour railway station stick to the water-side past the terminal for the car ferry to Friedrichshafen. A surfaced path runs next to the train track for 30min to

Rounding the point at Arbon

Egnach and its station. Proceed E through fields between the lake and the railway for the last leg via the Wiedenhorn baths and pretty parkland belonging to

2hr 15min – Arbon (398m). Across the bay SE appear the gentle green slopes of Rorschacher Berg, to be tackled tomorrow after a good night's rest. ⓘ (41) 071/4401380. Arbon is a charming town with shops, ATM, railway station, a photogenic castle and gabled houses. It also has a good choice of places to eat, and accommodation at homely Pension Sonnenhof ☎ (41) 071/4461510 **www.sonnenhof-arbon.ch** or waterfront Hotel Rotes Kreuz ☎ (41) 071/4461918 **www.hotelroteskreuz.ch**.

STAGE 2
Arbon to Rheineck

Time	3hr 45min
Distance	12.5km/7.7 miles
Ascent/Descent	160m/160m
Grade	1
Route profile	see Stage 1

This day is slightly shorter, with the E5 temporarily abandoning the lake to head inland through cultivated countryside as far as Goldach. Thereafter, all but bereft of waymarking, it involves a lengthy stretch of tarmac uphill to the scenic heights of Rorschacher Berg. Now for the good news – the modest mountain affords wonderful views over Lake Constance, and the concluding section is a leisurely stroll down to Rheineck for the night.

Leave **Arbon** (398m) via the waterfront promenade, shaded by chestnut trees, for the 15min stroll to **Steinach**. Yellow diamond signs for Goldach are plentiful, and initially you're led due S through a residential area. Lanes lead through farmland and orchards loaded with apples, grapes and cherries, then it's a short climb to traverse quiet **Tübach** (415m), before bearing SE along a stream to a covered bridge. Immediately afterwards turn R and follow signs carefully into the town of

1hr 15min – Goldach (449m). Shops, trains, ATM, modest Hotel Bahnhof ☎ (41) 071/8416690. 2.5km E on the lake's edge is the town of Rorschach ⓘ (41) 071/8417034 **www.tourist-rorschach.ch**.

Cross the road at the railway station and continue straight ahead on Neumühlstraße, which becomes Hohrainstraße. Houses are left behind and the motorway approached, but as views of the lake begin, signs soon point you L for Sulzberg. You dip briefly, veering R at a house for a path through woodland. This quickly emerges on a ridge and restaurant at **Sulzberg** (519m).

Downhill, near the motorway at crossroads, *ignore* waymarking and turn R for an underpass. This road climbs S to a bus stop marked St Anna Schloss. Go L through woods past overgrown castle ruins, then it's a gentle ascent with improving lake views. Quiet scenic roads take you E past **Schloss Wartensee** (560m, upmarket restaurant–hotel ☎ (41) 071/8587373 **www.wartensee.ch**), part of which dates back to the 12th century.

A little further on you cross a cog-wheel railway line and enter a beautiful beech wood. A path breaks off L downhill (Rheintal Höhenweg), rejoining the road shortly past farms. Cross a main road to take a narrow lane past a private manor and restaurant on the broad ridge of Buechberg (475m). The path that comes next gives delightful views, including neighbouring Rebensthal, where wine has been grown since the ninth century. Due N is a headland recognisable by an airstrip, and this is where the old course of the Rhine River drains into the lake.

At a panoramically positioned bar–restaurant, the way descends steeply to **Buriet** and inviting Gasthaus Schiff (☎ (41) 071/8884777 **www.schiff-buriet-rorschach.ch**). Turn R (S) for a short stroll along the main road to where it curves L (for the *Bahnhof* – railway station), but you walk straight on for

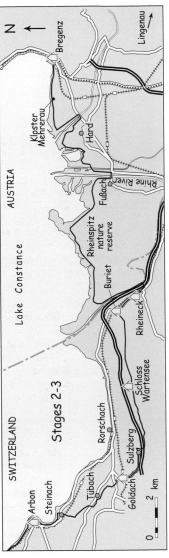

Arbon harbour backed by Rorschacher Berg

2hr 30min – Rheineck (399m) and cosy bed and breakfast Das Gasthaus ☎ (41) 071/8887268 **www.dasgasthaus.ch**. Also atmospheric *Altstadt* (old centre), with shops, ATM, restaurants and nondescript Hotel Hecht ☎ (41) 071/8882925.

STAGE 3
Rheineck to Lingenau

Time	5hr to Bregenz + 1hr by bus to Lingenau
Distance	27.7km/17.2 miles (on foot)
Ascent/Descent	Negligible
Grade	1
Route profile	see Stage 1
Map	see Stage 2

This last flat stage of the E5 is in Austria for the most part. The route around Lake Constance gives a fascinating insight into the hydrography of the mighty Rhine, as the river's outlets, natural and man made, are crossed, as is extensive reclaimed lowland, now the 2000-hectare Rheinspitz Nature Reserve, with its profusion of waterfowl and birds of prey. The latter part of the day entails walking on surfaced road, and waymarking disappears completely for a while. What's more, the 1:50,000 map is not especially helpful, so do follow directions with extra care. The good news is that the lovely lakeside city and transport hub of Bregenz is at the day's end, with accommodation at every price level. However, it is advisable to reach the pretty inland village of Lingenau by evening (buses run all day all year) so that an early start can be ensured next morning.

From the railway station at **Rheineck** (399m) *Wanderweg* signs take you over the road bridge that crosses the motorway and Rhine canal, and out of Switzerland past the *Zolldamt* (customs point). Turn L into Austria and past a supermarket to reach the quiet road that runs WWN between the canal and lovely old farmhouses.

After a restaurant you bear R into the traffic-free nature reserve, then keep R again (E) on a gravel track that doubles as a cycleway. This runs along the raised

Swimming spot in the Rheinspitz Nature Reserve

Edged with rushes the embankment is perfect for spotting herons and swans, not to mention buzzards, black kites and hawks. There is also the odd beach for hardy bathers.

Poldersdamm embankment, punctuated by the occasional sluice gate. ◀ After a restaurant the track veers SE, with the vast outlook taking in the mountainous Voralberg region backing Bregenz.

At boat sheds, some 40min on, a canal is crossed at **Fußach** (398m) where you need to turn immediately R. Ahead is an imposing embankment topped by a curious narrow-gauge railway line. Turn R here to reach an important road bridge that leads L across a grassed riverbed, which carries overflow for the adjacent watercourse – at last

2hr 45min – the Rhine River (398m).

Over the other side, go L on the road flanking the embankment as far as modest **Fischerheim**, a dark-timber restaurant shaded by willow trees. After a lock and covered footbridge, stick to the cycle track (*Radweg*) NE for a succession of bridges around the Binnen-becken inlet. Cut across the parks in **Hard** to head L (due N) onto Hafenstraße, lined with boatyards.

At the end of the road it's R onto the cycle track through woods, rounding the point. Not far on, turn into

Covered bridge en route to Hard

the trees following signs for Schützenheim (a club house with Wilhelm Tell on the wall). Then it's R for a path that emerges at a cascading canal – the Bregenzer Aache this time – to be crossed by a road bridge. A final loop L (NW) leads round via the Achmündung (river mouth, 398m) and back to the pleasant wooded lakeside, as per signs for Bodenseeweg, due E now.

The extensive monastery **Kloster Mehrerau**, surrounded by paddocks, is an interesting landmark, but attention soon moves to the glittering array of yachts and motorboats in the marinas, and at last the extraordinary Festspielhaus looms. Set on the lake itself, with a magnificent natural backdrop, the Festspielhaus is the breathtaking stage for the midsummer opera festival that has been running for 50 years, with audiences of up to 5000 watch from land-based seating. It's only minutes R through the park and over a footbridge to the railway station and bus terminal of

2hr 15min – Bregenz (400m). ① (43) 05574/425250. Capital of the Vorarlberg region, which became a fully fledged part of Austria (as opposed to Tyrol) in 1918.

Curiously, the following year the population voted to join Switzerland, but the idea did not meet with the approval of either the Swiss or the Allies, so it was dropped. Picturesque old district, vast numbers of outdoor cafés, sophisticated eating, full range of accommodation, shops, trains, buses, ATMs, and even a casino.

Reached by a scenic 1hr bus trip, the quiet village of **Lingenau** (685m) lies ESE of Bregenz in the gentle hills of the Bregenzerwald, part of Austria's westernmost province, the Vorarlberg region, renowned for its cheeses and traditional costumes. ① (43) 05513/6321. Shops and a scattering of guesthouses, including Gasthof-Pension Adler ☎ (43) 05513/6367 **www.adler-lingenau.at**. ◄

Note The railway line from Bregenz, shown on maps, no longer functions.

STAGE 4
Lingenau to Staufnerhaus

Time	4hr 45min
Distance	15.2km/9.4 miles
Ascent/Descent	1150m/200m
Grade	2
Route profile	see Stage 1

This stage is constantly varied, even though it is not particularly long. Starting in rolling hills and woodland, it touches on rural villages before venturing up the beautiful Lecknertal pasture valley, asphalted at first. The E5 crosses into Germany and climbs to a beautifully placed hut, giving a taste of the mountains, albeit the modest Allgäuer range. Alternative overnight stops can be made at guesthouses in Hittisau, or the traditional Höfle farm. If the weather is bad, or to avoid the surfaced stretches, buses can be taken to Hittisau, and then even as far as Reute in Lecknertal if preferred.

Note Should the long ridge traverse in Stage 5 not be to your liking, or if the weather turns bad, by all means cut out Staufnerhaus. Instead, from Höfle proceed along Lecknertal, on easy farm tracks and roads, to Gunzesried at the end of Stage 5 – see map and route description 'Direct Link to Gunzesried' towards the end of this stage. Alternatively, there are additional views to be enjoyed if you take the 'Variant High Route to Staufnerhaus', that breaks off from Lecknersee – see below.

In the main square of **Lingenau** (685m) E5 signposting points N, up the steepest road past the fire station, yellow/white arrows showing the way out of the village past farms. A climb follows, essentially E (red paint markings), through beautiful beech woods and onto the ridge to join a forestry track across 995m **Rotenberg**.

Lingenau is located in the Bregenzerwald

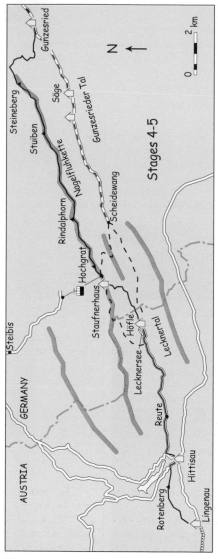

Keep a lookout for the turn-off R for Hittisau, which is a path that drops to the edge of the wood, giving inspiring views over villages and wooded valleys. At a junction for Häleisen at 820m, keep R and descend. You emerge on the road at a Y-intersection and proceed straight ahead for the *Ortsmitte* (town centre), namely the church and main square of

1hr 30min – Hittisau (790m)
ⓘ (43) 05513/6209. Shops, bus from Bregenz, accommodation such as Gasthof Krone ☎ (43) 05513/6201 **www.krone-hittisau.at**.

Turn L past Gasthof Krone, then shortly R at a shopping complex. Over a rise the path drops N to join the road and cross the Bolgernach watercourse, before a sharp turning R (E) for the start of the Lecknertal. It's 2km up the not unpleasant road to **Reute** (830m), the bus stop and popular local restaurant.

Not far up the road, a forest path provides a welcome if short alternative to the narrowing road, soon subject to a motorists' toll. Woodland alternates with rich pasture, key to the valley's proud dairy tradition, en route to the reed-lined lake

1hr 30min – Lecknersee (980m).

Variant High Route to Staufnerhaus (2hr 30min)
On the bottom edge of Lecknersee a signed path branches L (N) to climb via summer farms and a faint, narrow path to the crest. Here you turn R (E) towards the 1636m Hohenfluhalp elevation. The narrow, wooded crest is quite panoramic, but also exposed in places, not to mention slippery due to widespread mud after wet weather. A series of minor ups and downs leads to a saddle and **Staufnerhaus** (1634m).
Note This ridge route is only feasible in good weather.

The road continues uphill to the cosy farm-cum-modest guesthouse **Höfle** (1020m). ☎ (43) 05513/6535, mob (43) 0664/4956022. Sleeps 9, open late May to mid-October. Local cheese and smoked trout on sale.

Direct Link to Gunzesried (4hr 10min)
From the **Höfle** guesthouse in Lecknertal, head ENE, sticking to the farm track and crossing into Germany. Allow 2hr as far as the 1317m **Scheidewang** saddle (farm refreshments nearby) at the head of the Gunzesried valley. From here it's a further 7km/1hr 30min to the village of **Säge** (900m, accommodation, bus to Gunzesried), then 3km down the quiet road to Gunzesried. See the alternative descent route in Stage 5 for more details.

From **Höfle** the way narrows immediately to a gravel lane through beautiful pastureland. Very soon a signed track breaks off L (ENE), going over a stream and into woods where the Austrian–German border is crossed. Another watercourse is crossed, then there is a climb past farms. Cattle are everywhere, and their tracks can be confusing, but there are abundant red dots to guide walkers. ▸

A steep ascent N via **Lochalpe** (1419m) finally concludes at the superbly scenic crest Frangrat, not far from a cable-car lift. Only metres down the opposite side is

Underlying rock layers of conglomerate often show through, though there may also be a lot of mud.

1hr 45min – Staufnerhaus (1634m). Hospitable bustling DAV hut, sleeps 86, open May to early November, **www.staufner-haus.de**, fax ☎ (49) 08386/991121.

You can bail out by taking the Hochgratbahn cable-car down to connect with the daily bus to Steibis, and from there to Oberstaufen and rail links to Sonthofen and beyond.

STAGE 5
Staufnerhaus to Gunzesried

Time	7hr 30min
Distance	15.3km/9.5 miles
Ascent/Descent	600m/1350m
Grade	3
Map	see Stage 4

This is the first totally mountainous day of the E5, involving a lengthy traverse of the Nagelfluhkette ridge, with long exposed stretches and a taxing string of ups and downs. It is inadvisable in anything but perfect weather. The conglomerate rock and clay terrain are slippery when wet, which is not everyone's cup of tea, although there are multiple escape routes. Views are naturally wide-reaching and a brilliant array of Alpine flora can be admired. Plenty of drinking water and food is important today, as is sun protection, there being no shade until the very end. A lovely valley alternative, from Hochgrat via Scheidewang and Säge, is given if you want to avoid the ridge, and either way the stage concludes at a quiet rural village in traditional German Bavaria.

From **Staufnerhaus (1634m)** regain the crest of the Nagelfluhkette ridge via the wide track leading to the

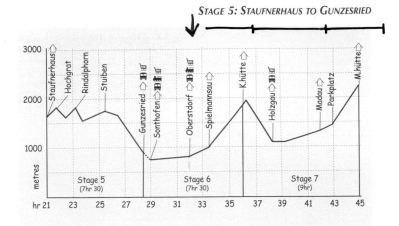

Hochgratbahn cable-car station. A straightforward valley alternative breaks off here.

Valley Alternative (4hr 30min)

From the cable-car station near Staufnerhaus, keep straight ahead in a gradually sloping descent E for Gleichenwangalpe, then along a track down to **Pass Scheidewang** (1315m, refreshments at nearby farm). Next, go due E along a quiet road (farm traffic only) through beautiful pastureland beneath the Nagelfluhkette ridge. A good way down there is an isolated farmhouse – Bergheim Waibel – offering accommodation and meals ☎ (49) 08321/4569. The next landmark is the village of **Säge** (900m), named after its sawmill, with inviting coffee bars and Alpengasthof Hirsch ☎ (49) 08321/2554. The final stretch is 40min on foot (or local bus) along the asphalt to **Gunzesried**.

Proceed carefully NE up the steep rocky crest to the cross on **Hochgrat** (45min, 1833m), a justifiably renowned lookout. Next, the E5 quickly loses height, heading for **Brunnenau Scharte** (1624m) and an escape route. The climb that follows starts on a narrowing path to reach the next peak

51

Nagelfluhkette seen from Säge

2hr 15min – Rindalphorn (1822m). The actual top involves a slight detour. It's not unusual to spot nimble chamois mountain goats on this precipitous terrain.

There is a drop of almost 300m, via a broad gully of loose rubble, to the next saddle, **Gündelesscharte** (1542m, escape route). This is followed by climbs via several minor peaks to

2hr 15min – Stuiben (1749m), a series of jagged oblique points, punctuated by scattered, lightning-struck larch trees (a short aided passage is involved). Mostly on the northern side of the ridge now, the path soon improves somewhat amidst grass cover with bright wildflowers.

1hr – Steineberg (1661m) is the final rock outcrop encountered on the Nagelfluhkette, with a marvellous outlook over the Alps of Bavaria. From now on it's all downhill, as you take your leave of the ridge.

At a marked junction for the Mittalberg lift, the E5 turns R (S) and soon joins a farm track to Vorder Krumbach Alpe farm (refreshments). It's not far down to

Traditional farm life at Vorder Krumbach Alpe

Dürrenhorn Alp, where a pretty path breaks off L through wood and meadows. Clear markings lead E and you soon emerge at the village store in

2hr – Gunzesried (889m). Delightful bed and breakfast Frau Beck ☎ (49) 08321/2915, or Gasthaus Goldenes Kreuz ☎ (49) 08321/2560; grocery shops, daily bus to Sonthofen.

STAGE 6
Gunzesried to Kemptnerhütte

Time	30min by bus to Sonthofen + 7hr
Distance	27km/16.7 miles (on foot)
Ascent	1100m
Grade	2–3
Route profile	see Stage 5

A short bus trip is followed by a leisurely stroll along the Iller river valley to the lively Alpine resort of Oberstdorf. The route then heads uphill into the attractive southernmost realms of the Allgäuer Alps and overnights at an exemplary Alpine hut on the E5's final day in Germany. This rather lengthy stage can be broken at either Oberstdorf, for those who enjoy a town atmosphere, or at the beautifully placed guesthouse at Spielmannsau in a quiet, pretty valley. On the other hand, walking times can be cut by taking a train or bus from Sonthofen to Oberstdorf, then either a horse and carriage (mornings only), or a less ecologically sound motorised taxi, up the road to Spielmannsau.

Note The uppermost part of the ascent to Kemptnerhütte is snow-bound well into the summer, necessitating a little extra care. However, the hut managers do their best to ensure a route is kept clear for visitors. If in doubt, check at the tourist office in Oberstdorf, or ring the hut hotline for the recorded message in German.

From **Gunzesried** a half-hour bus trip takes you to the valley floor and the railway station of the pleasant town of

30min – Sonthofen (742m) ① (49) 08321/615291. Train and buses in all directions, ATM, shops, accommodation.

Directly opposite the station take Bahnhofstraße E through the shopping area, then curve R through the pedestrian zone and the lovely old part of town. Marktstraße leads to the church and out near a castle as you head S, traversing the residential area on Frühlingsstraße. Then it's across the railway line and past the swimming pool.

Cut SW across the car park and continue past tennis courts to the gravel-based cycle track that follows the banks of the River Iller (30min). Turn L (S). The next stretch is shady at times and straightforward, giving you time to appreciate the snow-splattered mountains all around, especially if you make the most of the strategically placed picnic benches.

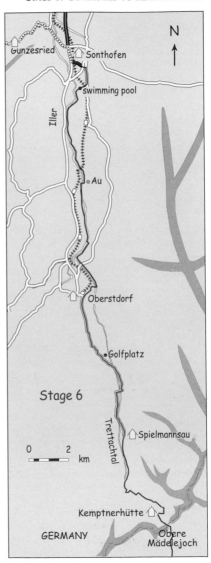

1hr on, near the village of **Au**, turn R across the bridge and join the cycle track on the opposite bank, going through pleasant forest alive with bird song. Cliffs begin to drawn in. About 1hr from Au take care not to miss the bridge that crosses back to the eastern side of the river. Not far on is the confluence of three watercourses – the Stillach, Trettach and Breitbach unite to become the Iller, the name originating in the ninth century when the river was known as the Hilaria. The Iller flows N to Ulm where it joins the Danube.

Curving SE you find yourself hugging the Trettach river and nearing the town. A while after a camping ground turn R over a bridge for the *Ortsmitte* (town centre), ignoring the *Bahnhof* (railway station) sign and continuing for the *Krankenhaus* (hospital). After the hospital head for the church in lovely traffic-free Marktplatz, the main square of

3hr – Oberstdorf (814m). The name comes from 'uppermost town', this being the southernmost corner of Germany. Developed as a mountain resort with a mild climate, it is characterised by buildings from the 19th century. ① (49) 0833/700217, ATM, accommodation, shops, buses and trains. Horse-drawn

Beautiful woods are traversed en route to Oberstdorf

carriages (*Stellwagen*) and taxis cover the narrow 7km road to Spielmannsau.

Note A local bus service also runs from the railway station as far as the golf links (*Golfplatz*) at the opening of the Trettachtal valley, a saving of 3km.

Leave the square on Prinzenstraße, a narrow lane that heads due S out of town. Approx 1km on, it joins Lorettostraße. At the ensuing forks, take care to follow signs for Spielmannsau and Trettachtal, bearing SE to the **Golfplatz** and car parks. Traffic for the final 4km is limited, so the going is pleasant.

1hr 30min – Spielmannsau (983m), guesthouse, restaurant and youth hostel ☎ (49) 08322/3015 **www.spielmannsau.de** (mini-bus available for guests).

A lane meanders S through the emerald green fields of Trettachtal, with the promise ahead of snowy mountains. After a modest *Jausenstation* (farm-cum-snack bar) and the goods lift for the hut ahead, a clear path takes over, going along the L bank of the stream. It steadily climbs high over the narrowing valley, through mixed conifer woods with martagon lilies and purple orchids. Several sidestreams and chutes channelling gravel mixed with old snow are crossed.

At the 1232m mark you turn L (SE) up the dramatic *Sperrbachtobel* gully and cross the watercourse twice. The valley tends to be choked with snow well into the

Striding out up Trettachtal

Snow-choked Sperrbachtobel gully preceding Kemptnerhütte

summer, necessitating care on the upper sections, especially if icy. Stick to the trodden trail and make use of your poles. A reassuring length of cable aids a passage hugging the rock face. The path finally emerges into a surprisingly green pasture basin, crowned by attractive peaks, and bears R (S) for the final climb to

2hr 30min – Kemptnerhütte (1846m). DAV, sleeps 290, open 15 June to 15 October **www.kemptner-huette.de**. Information hotline, ☎ (49) 08322/700152 (recorded message in German). Dating back to 1891, the comfortable building has been extended and modernised on many successive occasions. Sunsets are wonderful, and meals aren't bad either!

STAGE 7
Kemptnerhütte to Memmingerhütte

Time	9hr (or 2hr 20min to Holzgau + 1hr bus/taxi to Memmingerhütte Parkplatz + 2hr 10min)
Distance	23.3km/14.4 miles
Ascent/Descent	1250m/850m
Grade	2
Route profile	see Stage 5

A stunning Alpine stage back in Austria, with marvellous wide-reaching views and a wonderful hut at the day's end. The drawback is the length, though this can be reduced courtesy of the summer minibus/taxi service from Holzgau up the Madautal, a saving of 4hr 30min. Otherwise it is advisable to break the stage at either Holzgau or Madau hamlet, halfway up the valley.

Leave **Kemptnerhütte** (1846m) for the path SE uphill beneath the prominent Kratzer. ▸

20min – Obere Mädelejoch (1974m), a broad pass where the E5 leaves Germany for the last time to re-enter Austria amidst spreads of glacier crowfoot, and even ibex for early birds. Across the valley SE is the Ramstallspitze. Waymarking is red/white stripes from here on. The path is rocky but clear, and heads due S to descend Hohenbachtal, with carpets of Alpine wildflowers such as bright-blue bulbous gentian, bear's-ear primrose and pale-pink alpenrose.

The path drops to a basin to follow a torrential, crashing stream that cascades through a cleft gorge. A tiny shepherd's hut in a sea of dwarf mountain pine is reached, then the wood thickens and the descent becomes steeper.

The glorious grassy meadows are home to a thriving marmot colony, members of which feast enthusiastically on the wildflowers.

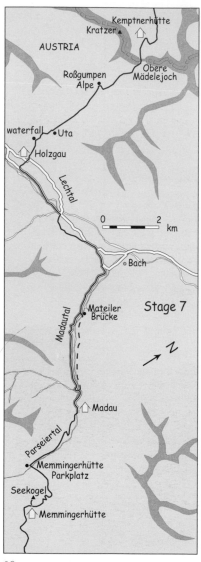

Down on the valley floor is the **Roßgumpen Alpe** café (1325m, 1hr), close to the foot of a waterfall. A farm road continues easily S. At **Jausenstation Uta** fork R for a gorge and the dramatic chute of Simmswasserfall. The waterfall is named after Sir Frederick R Simms, a turn-of-the-century London industrialist who spent years hunting in the Tyrol. His first visit was on the personal recommendation of Emperor Franz Josef.

The narrow, concrete-based track crosses back and forth beneath soaring vertical rock strata, to soon reach Lechtal and the neat white church of

2hr – Holzgau (1103m), a pretty Tyrolean farming village with frescoed houses. ⓘ (43) 05633/5356. Groceries, accommodation at bed and breakfast Haus ☎ (43) 05633/5394 or Gasthaus zum Bären ☎ (43) 05633/5217 **www.holzgau.net**. Minibus taxis will transport small groups the 13km up Madautal as far as the Memmingerhütte car park, otherwise the same family company runs a bus (mid-June to Sept) via the village of Bach to the same destination ☎ (43) 05633/5633.

Head S across the fields, then L (E) via a minor road along the River Lech. As the main road is reached the E5 branches off R, running parallel for a short way before rejoining the tarmac for the fork R at the opening of the Madautal valley (1hr this far). On the southern edge of a precipitous gully, the narrow road climbs steadily through mixed woodland.

Those with time to spare can cross the **Mateiler Brücke**, encountered at 1182m on the L (N) side of the Alperschonbach, to see the plunging Madau gorge. A path does continue on the northern bank to Madau, but the crumbly terrain makes it vulnerable to landslips, so check beforehand.

Otherwise stick to the narrow road to the turn-off for

3hr 30min – Madau (1310m), a traditional medium-altitude farming hamlet with its own chapel and Berggasthaus Hermine ☎ (43) 0664/5339770, open May to Oct.

With just 3km left on the now unsurfaced road, going through steep-sided Parseiertal, it's only

1hr – Memmingerhütte Parkplatz (1454m) and the hut's goods-lift loading point. Walkers can entrust their rucksack to the lift for a small fee, payable on arrival, although the sign specifies '*Keine Haftung*', meaning 'no responsibility taken'.

Taking it easy en route to Memmingerhütte

The rough though blinding scree is brightened by leopard's-bane as you move into a limestone zone.

A clear path strikes out E, winding relentlessly uphill through dense vegetation (the flora includes orchids and martagon lilies). A good 350m up, the path moves into a lovely expanse of pasture fed by waterfalls. Criss-crossing streams, the path now needs to climb around the impressive outcrop of Seekogel. ◀ It's a steep haul up into the next marvellous level, a glorious, glacially shaped basin, a world of its own, appreciated by the Haflinger horses left to graze freely here. Although the hut doesn't come into view until the very last moment, the last leg is a pleasant stroll S across a flowery meadow to the magnificent setting of welcoming

2hr 10min – Memmingerhütte (2242m) ☎ (43) 05634/6208, fax (43) 05634/20036. DAV, sleeps 142, open 12 June to 25 September. Spotless dorms and modern bathrooms.

Seekogel Sidetrip (1hr return)
Try to conjure up the energy to pop up the neighbouring 2412m Seekogel. The 360° views are breathtaking.

The beautiful surrounds of Memmingerhütte

STAGE 8
Memmingerhütte to Zams

Time	5hr 15min
Distance	13km/8 miles
Ascent/Descent	357m/1832m
Grade	2–3

Easily one of the most spectacular stages on the E5 so far, Stage 8 is incredibly varied, with brilliant Alpine scenery and wild valleys. A strenuous climb to a scenic high-altitude pass is followed by a steady and problem-free descent down a forested pasture valley, which narrows to a deep, intriguing ravine. Make sure you have an abundant supply of food and drinking water, and take your time, as this stage is too beautiful to rush. Only the initial section is steep and a little tricky. The day's destination is Zams, a welcoming small town on the River Inn in Austria, with a full range of services, and excellent accommodation, food and transport options.

From the **Memmingerhütte (2242m)** and its generator head SE across the magnificent amphitheatre, taking care to follow the signs for Zams. This involves a swing L along the lower Seewi lake's marshy NE edge for a broad gully climb E across rubble and mud, covered by inevitable tongues of snow. ▶ Half an hour up, watch out for a junction where you keep L (SE) for the final tiring scree slope, high above ice-bound tarns. A short hands-on clamber via an easy chimney brings you out at panoramic

Where the grass runs out, lilac penny cress and glacier crowfoot provide colour.

1hr 15min – Seescharte (2599m), a cleft pass between Seescharten Spitze and a curious jagged ridge that goes by the name of Schweinrücken (hog back), home to a sizeable herd of ibex which apparently find relaxation on the most arduous crags.

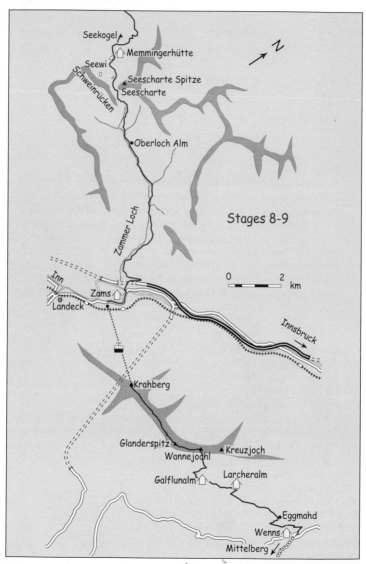

View to Memmingerhütte during the climb to Seescharte

At your feet a clear path heads down a vast valley that extends due E, backed by the Venetberg. (Ignore the fork L for Wurttemberger Haus.) The upper section is a magnificent rugged amphitheatre streaked with snow. ▶ Dwarf mountain pines anchor the terrain, and grassy flanks are soon approached, studded with gentians, striated daphne and clumps of pretty pink alpenrose, well watered by numerous streams.

The valley floor is finally gained, and a little further along is Oberloch Alm (1799m), with a drinking fountain. The gradient has eased considerably now, and the path continues on flat ground along the L side of the

Take care, as the loose scree makes for a knee-jarring descent, the going relentless to say the least.

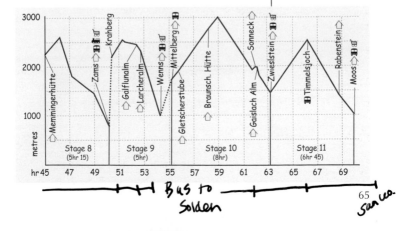

Nearly there! The path overlooks Zams and the Inn river

Lochbach and into conifer woods. The stream is crossed several times and a modest farm (with wildly overpriced refreshments) passed.

After a brief uphill stretch over a lip, the landscape changes dramatically as the E5 bears S to enter a dramatic ravine, the **Zammer Loch**. A clear though somewhat narrow cliff-hugging path is cut into the limestone flank, and wends its way carefully down this dizzily steep-sided valley, with the stream crashing along hundreds of metres below. (Spare a thought for the farmers who herd their cows up here!) Arolla pines with red trunks cling to the cliffs.

The main Inn valley can soon be seen ahead, with the transport hub of Landeck. However, you gradually round a corner bearing E and slowly but surely descend in zigzags. At last Zams comes into view, surrounded by a photogenic patchwork of green fields and the sparkling meanders of the River Inn, backed by the Venet massif, tomorrow's route. A dirt track on the valley floor is finally gained, and a sign points you R to cross the motorway (in a tunnel here) and reach a chapel. Continue along the road and across the River Inn towards the church at

4hr – Zams (775m) on the Via Claudia Augusta, an ancient Roman way. ① (43) 05442/63395, buses and trains, ATM, shops. Restaurants, hotels and guesthouses including bed and breakfast Haus Kurz ☎ (43) 05442/62841 and Postgasthaus Gemse ☎ (43) 05442/62478 **www.gasthof-gemse-haueis.at**.

STAGE 9
Zams to Mittelberg

Time	10min cable-car + 4hr to Wenns + 50min by bus to Mittelberg
Distance	12.5km/7.7 miles (on foot)
Ascent/Descent	750m/1550m
Grade	2
Route profile	see Stage 8
Map	see Stage 8

A relatively leisurely stage, thanks to the cable-car that conveys you effortlessly up to the 2200m mark, and a gentle ascent along a brilliantly panoramic crest. (**Hint** Get your guesthouse to stamp the *Venetbahn* brochure to ensure discounted fares.) Two modest farms in scenic spots offer simple accommodation and meals en route as an alternative to the towns.

To leave **Zams (775m)** head for the *Venetbahn*, a 5min stroll S of the town centre. It's a treat riding the cable-car up to 2200m **Krahberg**, a popular lookout offering refreshments and 360° views. Take time to survey the route you covered yesterday – the narrow cleft of the valley of Zammer Loch seems impenetrable!

A cluster of yellow signs includes Wenns and E5, and red/white striped markers show the way due E along

On the ridge from Krahberg

a wide, grassy crest of metamorphic origin, bright with heather. A gentle climb sees you at

1hr – Glanderspitz (2513m), with a prominent cross. Not far along the crest the E5 turns down R at 2497m **Wannejochl** (a little way below a second cross and Kreuzjoch). Descending SE, it traverses peaty terrain, with thick, springy carpets of heather and alpenrose, as well as soft cotton grass, wild chives, and bistort where it's marshy.

After summer farm **Galflunalm** (near Krugerhütte on maps, 1961m), ☎ (43) 0676/3837212 for basic meals and accommodation, an easy farm track leads E to a similar sleep-and-eat establishment, **Larcheralm** ☎ (43) 0664/5100990.

The lovely path leads beneath beautiful conifers that are home to noisy nutcrackers, with bilberry shrubs underfoot.

In wide curves the track drops down through pine forest, then a path soon breaks off R, signed for Wenns. ◀ There are views S down the Pitztal valley and to your next destination. You short-cut the track several times (not shown on the Kompass map), and cross meadows on a path marked in red, leading E straight down to dairy farms. The 'Alter Almweg' ('old herding route') is followed

Glanderspitz

briefly, then a road is joined to descend past the farm-houses of **Eggmahd** and Haus Venetblick.

At an intersection (where the track from Larcheralm joins up), recognisable by a mapboard and chapel, turn R downhill to

3hr – Wenns (982m) ⓘ (43) 05414/86999. Buses to Mittelberg (or taxis if you miss the former), groceries and an inviting cluster of coffee shops, several with beautifully frescoed walls. Accommodation includes Ferienhaus Wenns ☎ (43) 05414/87215 **www.sailer-hotels.at**.

Note If the weather is threatening to turn bad, or the high-altitude ascent awaiting in Stage 10 is not to your liking, then take a bus N to nearby Imst. From Imst there is a connection down the parallel Ötztal and past Sölden to Zwieselstein. Here you can pick up the E5 again at Stage 11. On the other hand, should you reach Wenns in time for the early afternoon bus to Mittelberg, and feel the urge to keep walking, by all means embark on the ascent to Braunschweiger Hütte. A 30min stroll uphill brings you to the Gletscherstube, with dormitory accom-modation and simple meals (see Stage 10).

Mittelberg (1734m) at the southernmost end of the road along Pitztal is a cluster of hotels dwarfed by vast glacial valleys, headed by the awesome 3773m Wildspitze. Accommodation possibilities include classy hotel Gletscherblick ☎ (43) 05413/86292 **www.gletscherblick.at**, or with a star or 2 less, Berghof Steinbock ☎ (43) 05413/86238 **www.berghof-steinbock.at**.

STAGE 10
Mittelberg to Zwieselstein

Time	8hr
Distance	19.8km/12.3 miles
Ascent/Descent	1320m/1600m
Grade	3
Route profile	see Stage 8

A memorable stage with a tremendous climb to a superb pass high above breathtaking glaciers, at 2995m the highest point on the whole of the E5. Good weather with clear visibility is obviously preferable simply because of the panoramic views to be enjoyed. But more seriously, the high-altitude passage over the Pitztaler Jöchl has exposed stretches, and it can be slippery and potentially treacherous. Under no circumstances should it be attempted in anything but perfect weather conditions. Afterwards there is a prolonged but very scenic traverse of woodlands and fields, concluding at a peaceful village. This is the renowned Ötztal, dominated by high peaks draped with glaciers and snow fields.

Note This stage is rather too long for enjoyment, but thanks to the marvellous high-altitude Braunschweiger Hütte it can be broken up into more manageable chunks. There are also guesthouses during the latter part of the descent.

Leave **Mittelberg (1734m)** on the broad dirt road SE. It goes along a perfect U-shaped valley where a stream, cloudy with ice-melt, clatters along. ▶

30min – Gletscherstube (1891m) is a friendly restaurant with dorm and kitchen facilities ☎ (43) 0664/3944118, open May–October, and sleeps 16. Shuttle service available from Mittelberg **www.gletscherstube.at**.

Close by is the loading point for the Braunschweiger Hütte's goods lift – rucksacks can be added for a modest

The stark surrounds of red-grey rock slopes are dotted with the odd tree, but the gaze is drawn ahead to rugged rock points, at whose feet a tongue of ice peeks through.

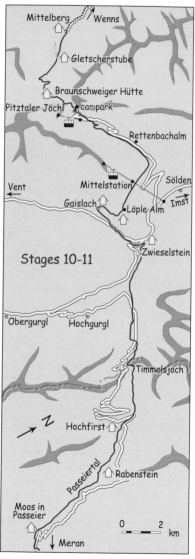

Mittelberg

Wenns

Gletscherstube

Braunschweiger Hütte

Pitztaler Jöchl — car park

Rettenbachalm

Mittelstation

Sölden

Vent

Gaislach

Löple Alm

Imst

Zwieselstein

Stages 10-11

Obergurgl

Hochgurgl

Timmelsjoch

N

Hochfirst

Passeiertal

Rabenstein

Moos in Passeier

0   2 km

↓ Meran

fee (you need to tell them by phone), though no responsibility for them is accepted.

The path heads uphill on the L bank of a gushing torrent to a series of glacially smoothed rock slabs and thundering waterfalls. The surrounds are simply magnificent, and extensive moraine ridges creep slowly outwards. A stiff ascent approaches the glacier snout, accompanied by improving views over the vast blue-grey extensions of the glacier, beneath towering mountains such as the Wildspitze. Rock slab steps lead inexorably upwards, curving under the lift cable, swinging E to superbly placed

2hr 30min – Braunschweiger Hütte (2759m) ☎ (43) 0664/5353722, DAV, **www.braunschweiger-huette.at**, open mid-June to end September, sleeps 120, and dates back to 1892. A terrace overlooks the glacier spread, while inside guests are warmed by the traditional *Stube*, a ceramic-coated stove.

With clear red/white markings, the E5 now heads NNE across late-lying snow and loose rock on the ascent up the ridge at the rear of the hut. It's quite surprising to find moon daisies and yellow cinquefoil flourishing at these altitudes. A narrowish saddle with multi-coloured rock (and probably snow) is traversed, before a hands-on clamber across an exposed stretch (slippery if wet).

Only metres away now is
45min – Pitztaler Jöchl (2995m), at the foot of Karles Kogel, a breathtaking on-top-of-the-world pass overlooking Austria's renowned Ötztal and its ample year-round ski fields.

The E5 climbs high above Braunschweiger Hütte and the glacier

A steep snowfield descent awaits. It will hopefully be a matter of soft snow, so put on your gaiters and dig in your heels. The direction is essentially NE. About 40min will see you at a **car park**.

Exit to Sölden
Keep R down the road for the Rettenbach cable-car station and summer-long bus for the resort of **Sölden** ① (43) 05254/510, from where there are connections for Zwieselstein.

The E5 drops on a clear path to a chapel before cutting across the private toll road that brings year-round skiers from the valley floor and Sölden. You're soon well

73

*Snowfield below
Pitztaler Jöchl*

Café/restaurant
Rettenbachalm
(2145m) is a useful
landmark (much
mentioned on
signposts).

below the level of the glaciers, following Rettenbachtal valley and its stream E, soon crossed as you join a wide service track. The surroundings are still stark, though there is a noticeable increase in wildflowers, such as alpine mouse-ear, and there are even grazing cows. ◄ A short stretch of tarmac, then you branch R across beautiful, gently sloping flanks thick with alpenrose. The path runs parallel to the main Ötztal, backed by an attractive line-up of peaks, including the snow-plastered point of Zuccherhutl N. There are slight uphill sections through juniper and Arolla pine, a couple of winter ski pistes are crossed, and you pass under the Gletscherbahn cable-car not far from the **Mittelstation**. The E5 route is well marked and soon reaches welcome

2hr 45min – Löple Alm (1912m), where refreshments can be enjoyed on a terrace with panoramic views towards Timmelsjoch, on tomorrow's route.

It's a brief climb to a saddle, then guesthouse Alpengasthof Sonneck ☎ (43) 05254/2905. Turn R (W) along the farm road past Almgast Gaislach Alm ☎ (43) 05254/2914 **www.gaislachalm.com**. Very soon you

need to branch L on a gravel road, and at last the descent down the northern flanks of the pretty Venter Tal begins in earnest. Several short cuts present themselves, but it's not far to the photogenic hamlet of **Gaislach** (1793m), with its geranium-bedecked houses and tiny domed church.

Tiny hamlet of Gaislach

Now a zigzagging path plunges E into conifer woods, welcomingly soft underfoot, to later emerge on tarmac. Go L on the surfaced road to where a path breaks off R, following the crashing river that conveys the meltwater from the mighty Similaun glacier at the head of the Vent valley.

1hr 30min – Zwieselstein (1450m) ('split rock'). Pleasant village with groceries, buses along Ötztal, plenty of good value places to eat and bed and breakfasts, such as Haus Holzknecht ☎ (43) 05254/2993 or Gasthof Brückenwirt ☎ (43) 05254/2769. There is dormitory accommodation and self-catering at the comfortable DAV Talhütte, custodian ☎ (43) 05254/2763, sleeps 35, open year-round, bookings c/o **www.alpenverein-regensburg.de**. Nearest tourist office is at Sölden.

STAGE 11
Zwieselstein to Moos in Passeier

Time	6hr 45min
Distance	19km/11.8 miles
Ascent/Descent	1059m/1502m
Grade	2
Route profile	see Stage 8
Map	see Stage 10

A final section in Austria, then the E5 enters Italy once and for all, though little changes initially, as this is the South Tyrol. This is a pretty long stage, opening with a stiff climb to the Timmelsjoch pass and the Austrian–Italian border. A relentless descent follows – initially via stark terrain, then picturesque farming valleys – to comfortable accommodation in a well-placed village.

At the start, the road that climbs to Timmelsjoch is subject to a toll for motorists. Of greater interest to walkers, however, is the bus that runs up the pass every day in midsummer, a boon for those weary after the rigours of Stage 10, as it cuts off 3 hours' walking. Accommodation in the pretty hamlet of Rabenstein is a useful alternative during the descent, as is Hochfirst, a minimal detour off the main route.

Uphill from the grocery store in **Zwieselstein** (1450m) the E5 turns L (SE) up a lane following a stream, and quickly leaves the houses behind. Soon becoming a path, it's a steady, well-signed (red/white) climb through conifer woods. Orchids abound, as do house-leeks on sun-baked rocks. A deep gorge separates the walkers' route from the road.

The settlement of Obergurgl comes into view S, with a backdrop of glaciated mountains. Bearing E, you emerge on heathland, and around halfway in terms of altitude, cross an ageing timber bridge over the crystal-clear, non-glacial stream. The path continues parallel to the road, which is subsequently crossed twice between marshy terrain. You return to the L bank of the Timmelsbach stream at the 2100m mark for a steep climb towards a crest, in the company of bilberries, marmots and sheep. Set in undulating grassy terrain with wide-ranging views, you come out at the road at

3hr – Timmelsjoch/Passo del Rombo (2509m), the Austrian–Italian border since 1918. The name is derived from old Roman for 'hill', and was used by generations of shepherds en route to high summer pastures with their flocks. Wooden 'shack-cum-souvenir-shop-cum-pricey-snack-bar' with hot food, popular with cyclists and bikers. On the Italian side the road has been open to motorists since 1968, but is unbelievably tortuous and narrow, and kept snow-free only between June and October. The pass is a significant watershed: rain that lands on the eastern side will end up in the Adriatic Sea, whereas if it happens to fall on the western-facing slope, it will flow into the Black Sea.

From the actual border a clear path breaks off SE, via stone steps down a rock-strewn mountainside, passing ruined buildings in a vast, stark, rounded valley – Passeirer Timmelstal. Things green up as you descend, and marmots appear. Now in the Texel Nature Park, at 1960m there is a turn-off for the guesthouse Hochfirst (☎ (39) 0473/647040). Just a brief detour brings you to its scenic position on the road from Timmelsjoch. The main route is easily rejoined in the valley directly below the building.

You soon join the road and reach a bridge and a dramatic ravine, and not far afterwards a path breaks off R to thread through traditional-style farms, with an old mill on the riverside. A bridge crosses to the R bank on a forestry track through a steep-sided valley with farmhouses perched crazily on impossibly steep mountainsides. A final short cut and you join a minor road into photogenic

2hr 30min – Rabenstein/Corvara in Passiria (1420m), the name a reference to crows. Snack bars, limited groceries,

Gasthof Rabenstein ☎ (39) 0473/647000 and Gasthof Trausberg ☎ (39) 0473/647055. A good base for visiting the Schneeberg mines NE, which claim to be the highest in Europe, and at 2500m the most elevated permanent settlement, as well as the world's longest quarrying conveyor-belt system (27km), where over 60 different minerals were extracted from the 13th century up until 1967.

Stick to the road for 30min. As it veers L uphill, turn off R for the path along the river, strewn with curious hunks of marble and red rock. The valley narrows considerably, and there may be the odd detour due to rock falls. Opposite the imposing Weisspitz outcrop, a lane leads you straight into the peaceful Alpine village of

1hr 15min – Moos in Passeier/Moso in Val Passiria (1007m), which comes from 'marsh'. ⓘ (39) 0473/643558. ATM, supermarket, daily buses via St Leonhard to Meran. Accommodation, including Cafè Maria ☎ (39) 0473/643563, with comfortable rooms and inexpensive food. The Passeiertal is distinguished by record rainfall levels and unstable rocky terrain – no wonder it is prone to landslides and seasonal flooding.

STAGE 12
Moos in Passeier to Pfandleralm

Time	5hr
Distance	15km/9.3 miles
Ascent/Descent	1030m/690m
Grade	1–2

The E5 spends the whole day in the beautiful farming region of Passeiertal, traversing woods on age-old pathways and offering a precious glimpse into traditional rural life. After climbing 300m to Stulles, it drops to the lively township of St Leonhard, only to embark on another stiff climb at day's end, but the reward is worthwhile, as Pfanderalm is a lovely place to stay. To shorten the day, by all means catch the bus to St Leonhard.

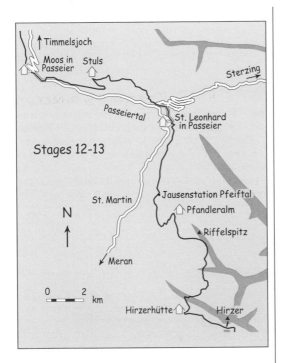

From the intersection near the tourist office, walk out of **Moos in Passeier** (1007m) via the main road. Immediately after a short tunnel the E5 forks l (F) up a narrow, stepped path into beautiful woods with the odd farm, complete with ingenious cableway systems. About 1hr along at a cluster of houses keep L on the surfaced road uphill for the quiet village of

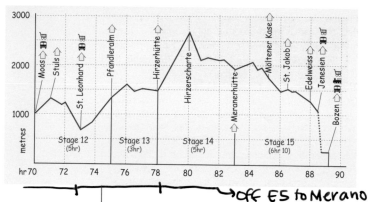

hr 70   72   74   76   78   80   82   84   86   88   90

→ *off E5 to Merano*

Village in Passeiertal

1hr – Stulles/Stuls (1332m) and wonderful views S up the Plan valley. Accommodation includes Café-Pension Gufler ☎ (39) 0473/649547 **www.pensiongufler.com**.

Keep R (E) along the road and past an old shrine to where a marked path turns R. Follow waymarks and signs carefully SE through woods, past waterfalls and across fields with bird's-eye views of the township at the foot of

Plattenspitz. A short stretch of road is followed by a plunge through chestnut woods to Gruberhof farm. The next useful landmark is a sawmill, then a road going downhill. Go L at the intersection (sign for Meran) into the centre of

2hr – St Leonhard in Passeier/San Leonardo in Passiria (693m) ① (39) 0473/656188. Buses to Meran, ATM, cafés and hotels galore. This is a good place to stock up on food, as the next shops are at the end of Stage 15. This was the birthplace of Andreas Hofer, the local hero who led the 1809 resistance against Napoleon in the South Tyrol, and a museum in his memory can be visited.

Walk through the town to the picturesque river bridge complete with picnic benches. Overlooking the main square next to the river is geranium-bedecked Hotel Strobler – the E5 takes the road alongside the hotel and climbs past the Volkschule, heading S away from the built-up area. A delightful path takes over, going through cool woods where ancient irrigation channels are encountered en route to a waterfall. The path then coasts into inviting **Jausenstation Pfeiftal**, above the village of

Descent towards St Leonhard

St Martin, and where fresh yoghurt and homemade cakes can be enjoyed (though over-indulgence is inadvisable in view of the imminent climb!).

A shady if steep route now leads SE through raspberry-laden woods via farms to the Pfandlerhof Gasthof and a superb outlook over Passeiertal. The path (waymarked n.1) turns R to the rear of this building, crossing meadows and intersecting a forestry track. Dark conifer woods and a punishing paved way characterise the last leg to the idyllic location of

2hr – Pfandleralm (1350m) ☎ (39) 0473/641841, sleeps 16, open May to October (May–June closed Mondays). A friendly, comfortable place with a perfect shower, al fresco dining and chilled beer. 'Pfand' means 'pledge', and Pfandleralm is of great symbolic importance to the whole of the Tyrol, as the patriot Andreas Hofer was arrested here in 1810 by French troops.

STAGE 13
Pfandleralm to Hirzerhütte

Time	3hr
Distance	6.5 km/4 miles
Ascent/Descent	820m/200m
Grade	2–3
Route profile	see Stage 12
Map	see Stage 12

A fairly short stage, this is a perfect, not to mention well-earned, semi-rest day, or it is easily combined with the following stage, weather and fitness permitting. In all it is a delightful walk with superb views. The odd narrow, exposed stretch is involved, requiring extra care especially in wet weather.

Note Due to landslips, on the initial stretch the E5 has been rerouted to a lower path, not shown on the Kompass map at the time of writing.

From **Pfandleralm** (1350m) take path n.1 across the meadow, past the old timber hut with Tyrolean banners (site of Andreas Hofer's arrest) and into forest. Forestry tracks traverse a partially reconstructed mountainside with landslip barriers, followed by a constant climb due S. There is the occasional hut and clearing, and views are ever improving.

The path emerges on open mountainside with wonderful views to the Brenta Dolomites S, the glaciated Ortler group SW and the Weisskugel NW. The stretch that follows is considerably narrower and can be slippery if wet. The climb continues to the 2100m mark, contouring E below Riffelspitz before curving into a basin under Kreuzjoch, popular with grazing goats. The path runs consistently above the tree line, across mountain flanks dotted with pink alpenrose shrubs and the triffid-like house-leek, and there are dizzy views to the valley floor.

A rock corner is rounded and you reach the summer farms Mahdalm and Hintereggalm (1990m), offering outdoor refreshments and popular with deckchair-bound tourists on sunny days. A broad farm lane leads SE into the next pasture basin, dominated by soaring Hirzer.

During the traverse to Hirzerhütte

Hirzerhütte backed by Hirzer

3hr – Hirzerhütte (1983m) ☎ (39) 333/3687429, sleeps 40, open mid-May to October. Booking advisable in August. Marvellous, rambling old-style family-run establishment with adjacent farm. Built in 1873, it is the work of dedicated members of the German and Austrian Alpine Club. Fresh dairy products are served, as is the best *apfelstrudel* on the E5! Expect rollicking live accordian music on a midsummer Sunday afternoon.

Exit to Meran
A 10min stroll away S at Klammeben is a cable-car link (Hirzer Seilbahn) with Salteis in Passeiertal, from where it is a short bus trip to Meran. ⓘ (39) 0473/272000, shops, hotels, bus and train services, and a charming town centre.

STAGE 14
Hirzerhütte to Meranerhütte

Time	5hr
Distance	9.4km/5.8 miles
Ascent/Descent	770m/825m
Grade	2–3
Route profile	see Stage 12

Opening with a steady climb and optional peak, this is a marvellous day's walking across a stunning ridge and peaceful, isolated cirques harbouring pretty lakes. Although one of the E5's top days, it is inadvisable in adverse weather conditions because of exposed rocky tracts. The day ends at a small-scale ski resort with a choice of accommodation.

From **Hirzerhütte** (1983m) the E5 – alias path n.4 – heads E past a goat farm then via a sequence of flowery natural terraces where marmots play. The grass gives way to rockier terrain, dotted with useful marker cairns, where saxifrage grows. On a rapidly steepening gradient you veer R (ESE) for a hands-on clamber up rocky passages, exposed in places. Follow the red/white paint splashes carefully up to the ridge and to

2hr – Hirzerscharte aka Obere Scharte/Giogo Piatto (2678m), a broad metamorphic saddle dotted with large cairns. Be prepared for 360° views (almost): in the foreground are the Sarntaler crests, then SE the spectacular Dolomites, including the crazy Odle – a series of jagged needles – and the fortress Sella. Stretching out SW is the glaciated Ortler–Cevedale range. Should these not be enough for you, by all means embark on the following (Grade 3) route to the summit.

Turn L along the ridge in the direction of Hirzer to a fork – turn R (E) in descent.

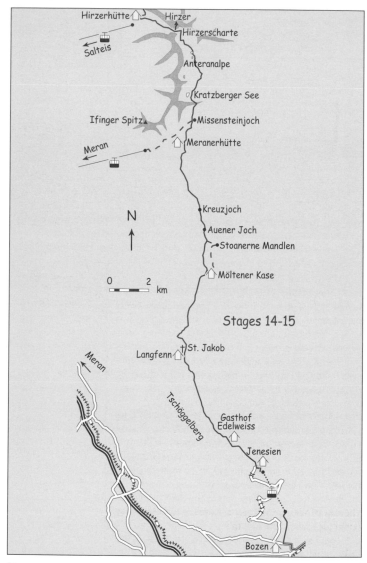

Ascent to Hirzerscharte

Optional Ascent to Hirzer/Punta Cervina (40min return)
From the fork, keep straight on (L) for the clear but constantly exposed route, climbing the final metres to spectacular 2781m Hirzer and its summit cross. Experienced walkers only – definitely no vertigo sufferers! Return the same way.

The path drops through a series of attractive cirques, populated by marmots and sheep amidst alpenrose shrubs. About 1hr below the ridge are small, pretty lakes in a granite setting, at Anteralpe. Turn sharp R (S) for a lengthy contour over streams and rock slabs, then it's uphill again to the 2100m mark with more brilliant views, such as the snowy Hochfeiler peak NE on the Austrian–Italian border. A couple of crumbly gullies are traversed as you round Kratz Berg, then endless curves before finally arriving at inviting

2hr – Kratzberger See/Lago di San Pancrazio (2119m), rather too chilly for a dip, though the water is home to tadpoles and fish of sorts. In the shadow of Verdinser Platten Spitz this is the perfect picnic spot.

Final stretch of ascent to Hirzerscharte, with Hirzer in the background

Kratzberger See

Continue on the narrowing path SE that makes its way around the eroding mountainside and yet more gullies to **Missensteinjoch (2128m)** and a clutch of signposts.

Exit to Meran
A path breaks off R (SW) to the Ifinger cable-car (30min). Down on the valley floor it's a short bus trip to the lovely town of Meran, ⓘ (39) 0473/272000, which offers plenty of accommodation, shops, bus and train services.

The E5 now enters the Meran 2000 ski complex, though in summer it involves gently sloping grassy slopes populated by grazing Haflinger horses, native to the area. A dirt road is joined to

1hr – Meranerhütte (1930m), AVS ☎ (39) 0473/279405, sleeps 70, open year-round. Vast terrace, and spotless if rather impersonal premises, with unreliable showers. A cosier option is nearby Kirchsteiger Alm ☎ (39) 0473/279609.

STAGE 15
Meranerhütte to Bozen

Time	6hr + 10min cable-car
Distance	24.8km/15.4 miles (on foot)
Ascent/Descent	254m/1134m
Grade	1–2
Route profile	see Stage 12
Map	see Stage 14

While rather long, this concluding stage of Part One is simply brilliant, with nothing at all in the way of technical difficulties, leaving walkers free to enjoy the marvellous emerging scenery – dominated by the glorious Dolomites. The route runs constantly above the tree line, with a good chance of observing numerous birds of prey. En route there is a string of welcoming refreshment places, as well as alternative accommodation. Though the stage ends in the city of Bozen, it's more pleasant to overnight in peaceful, medium-altitude Jenesien, which boasts excellent guesthouses and restaurants, then travel down the next morning by bus or cable-car for sightseeing and the continuing route.

Leave **Meranerhütte** (1930m) S on wide path n.4/E5 via a saddle, continuing uphill to reach a broad sandstone crest. Views in all directions are amazing, with highlights such as the Marmolada glacier SE and the Ortler group W.

After an unnamed pass with an artistic crucifix, you follow the fence in the company of cows for the gradual climb to **Kreuzjoch** (2084m), then continue on mostly level terrain via a series of signed junctions, including

1hr 30min – Auener Joch (1924m) and a recommended detour, for which timing is the same as for the main route.

Stoanerne Mandlen

Detour via Stoanerne Mandlen ('stone men', 2003m)
Leave the main E5 route for the clear signed path that climbs briefly SE to a neighbouring hill. Here there is a curious three-pronged cross and remarkable line-up of heaped-up stone cairns, some evidently dating back to prehistoric times. Proceed due S along the wide crest, then downhill past a feeding trough for the beautiful Haflinger horses that graze here. In the woods turn R at the junction to the farm restaurant of **Möltener Kase** (1763m) and the main route.

The E5 continues S, skirting the base of Stoanere Mandlen on a clear track to the fork L for

45min – Möltener Kase (1763m). A popular farm-cum-restaurant with bunk beds in the barn. ☎ (39) 368/400067, open May to early November.

The S direction is resumed on a broad farm track through woods – look out for the many forks and way-marking for the EFW5/n.4. Manicured parkland dotted

Elegant Haflinger horses graze freely

with trees is crossed to the accompaniment of ever-improving views to the Dolomites. The saddle at Möltener Joch (1734m) is passed, though you'd hardly know it. Further on, in a dip, there is a three-way road intersection where the E5 follows path n.1 straight up the other side to the gorgeous spot occupied by

1hr 15min – St Jakob (1525m), a photogenic Romanesque church and the Langfenn farm ☎ (39) 0471/668218, sleeps 15, always open.

A gravel lane leads SSE over more delightful undulating meadows and woods in this southern section of the Tschöggelberg plateau, known as Salten/Salto. Carefully maintained traditional timber fences mark properties, often occupied by tiny timber cabins originally built for use during haymaking, though many serve as holiday huts nowadays. ◀ This stretch is constantly pretty, if a little long.

The isolated larch trees were once harvested for their resin for commercial purposes.

As the lane finally begins to descend, a surfaced road takes over to 1360m and **Gasthof Edelweiss** ☎ (39) 0471/354106 **www.gasthof-edelweiss.com**, meals, accommodation, views and horse-riding.

Leave the road now for the red/white waymarked path through a delightfully cool wood of black pine. The church spire and rooftops of Jenesien, as well as the spread of the city of Bozen, come into sight. You emerge on the road (bus stop) and go straight over, heading downhill for the church and tourist office in the small square of

2hr – Jenesien/San Genesio (1087m). A lovely village clustered on a steep mountainside with a brilliant outlook. ① (39) 0471/354196. Accommodation ranges from charming 3-star Zum Hirschen ☎ (39) 0471/354195 **www.hirschenwirt.it** to good-value bed and breakfast Unterkofler ☎ (39) 0471/354149. ATM, shops, daily buses (30min trip) and cable-car (10min + 30min on foot) to Bozen.

At the bottom of the cable-car turn R along the road, then at the earliest opportunity go L to cross the Talvena river and join the delightful promenade. It's hard to imagine the widespread flooding and damage this placid watercourse has caused over the centuries. At the road bridge go L into the pedestrian centre of

40min – Bozen/Bolzano (262m). On Museumstraße you soon reach the archaeological museum, which houses the must-see Ice Man **www.archaeologiemuseum.it**. Proceed via the historic porticoed streets to Walther Platz and the tourist office, ① (39) 0471/307000, not far from the railway station and bus terminal. Plentiful shops, ATMs and accommodation, including a modern youth hostel ☎ (39) 0471/300865 **www.bozen.jugendherberge.it**.

The basin occupied by Bozen is, to say the least, sun blessed, and the inhabitants have been taking advantage of this to ripen their grapes since the first millennium BC. This inspiring description by Goethe after his 1786 journey is hard to better:

> *Girt by steep mountains which are cultivated up to a considerable height, it is open toward the south, but blocked to the north by the Tyrolean mountains. A mild, gentle air filled the region. Here the Adige turns south again. The hills at the foot of the mountains are planted with grapevines. The stocks are drawn over long, low arbors, from the tops of which the blue grapes hang down very prettily and ripen from the warmth of the ground.*

Butterloch canyon (Stage 16)

PART TWO
Bozen to Verona (14 days)

Now on the 'sunny side of the Alps' the E5 climbs high above the Adige river to head south through dense forest and traditional farming areas. Glorious views of the neighbouring Dolomite mountains are constant companions. Other highlights during the walk include an awesome ravine where running water has laid open millions of years' worth of geological strata.

German-speaking South Tyrol is soon left behind for Italian-speaking Trentino, and later on the Veneto region. However, dotted here and there are 'linguistic islands' – pockets of ancient German (Mocheno and Cimbro) at the foot of the rugged Lagoria mountains.

The Valsugana transport artery, a convenient place to join or leave the E5, precedes a return to higher altitudes. The beautiful Piccole Dolomiti range is explored, amidst poignant reminders of the tragedy of the First World War, which devastated these former border regions and scattered the population. Finally, all that separates walkers from a rewarding conclusion at Verona, romantic city par excellence, are the rolling hills of the Monti Lessini.

Vineyards around Segonzano castle (Stage 19)

STAGE 16
Bozen to Wastlhof

Time	10min cable-car + 8hr 5min
Distance	26.1km/16.2 miles (on foot)
Ascent/Descent	1050m/750m
Grade	2

A particularly full and varied stage that takes walkers through an exciting kaleidoscope of landscapes, initially traversing the vast porphyry plateau that surrounds Bozen. The start is a ride on a cable-car that glides over the treetops, above the sticky summer heat of the city, 262m above sea level, to a guaranteed cool, breezy 1135m. Further along the trail there is a peaceful sanctuary, then an amazing canyon, of great interest to geologists and non-geologists alike – allow plenty of extra time for exploration.

In view of the considerable length of this stage, and the many attractions en route, it is best to split it into shorter sections – there are numerous accommodation opportunities en route.

Bozen (262m) (see end of Stage 15 for tourist and accommodation details).

From the railway station turn NE along Via Renon, parallel to the tracks. Immediately after the Renon cable-car station the road drops below the railway and bears S as Via Piani di Bolzano then Via Macello. This soon crosses the River Isarco, and straight ahead, close to the motorway, is the departure station (20min) for the recently renewed Kohlern cable-car. A gently paced run (frequent daily service) will see you up at

30min – Kohlern/Colle (1135m), Bauernkohlern on many maps. The original cable-car, an open-sided

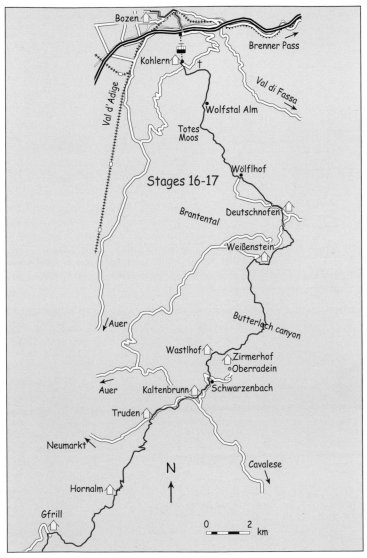

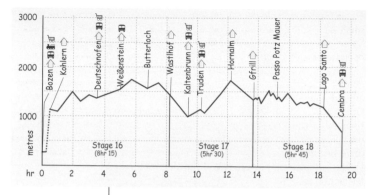

double-tiered bench affair (on display in the park) dates back to 1908. The brainchild of an enterprising local hotelier, it was the very first cable system in the whole of the Alps for passenger transport. Subject to modernisation on many occasions, the latest was in 2006, when the photogenic red cabins were replaced by state-of-the-art silver ones.

Bozen and Jenesien seen from Kohlern

▸ From the cable-car station turn R uphill past a small park and go around below a fairytale turreted house and guesthouse Klaushof ☎ (39) 0471/329999, open Easter to October.

Bearing E you need the gravel track/n.4 through conifer woods via a cluster of picturesque houses around a church at Herrenkohlern/Colle dei Signori. Due S now, a forestry track climbs gradually through silent forest with exquisite plays of light between slender conifer trunks, not to mention occasional glimpses of the beautiful Dolomite groups Catinaccio and Sciliar. Light refreshments are served at **Wolfstal Alm** ('wolf valley farm').

At the path junction of **Totes Moos**, a small nature reserve, turn L (SE) on n.1 to pass the marsh. A road is touched on briefly at a farm (Steiner), then n.1 plunges downhill and across the road. Thick patches of raspberry and bilberry shrubs accompany the descent to tarmac again, and you turn L for divinely positioned **Wölflhof** (1290m, 2hr 30min), a friendly outdoor café with brilliant Dolomite views and a dormant St Bernard dog.

Do take time to climb the nearby watchtower, an immense timber structure that gives stunning views over the entire Bozen basin and its mountainous surroundings – vineyards, glaciated peaks and all.

Dolomite views from Wölflhof

A short way down the road the E5/n.1-2 turns uphill steeply to a rise, and across pasture and woods with promising views S to the spires of the Weißenstein sanctuary backed by Weißhorn. Soon the Latemar massif appears SE. A short descent brings you to houses and a tarmac lane leading into the pretty village of

3hr – Deutschnofen/Nova Ponente (1357m), the name a reference to its founders, ancient Bavarian tribes who settled these uplands in the seventh century. ⓘ (39) 0471/616567, ATM, shops and guesthouses, including Pensione Rössl ☎ (39) 0471/616510. Buses to Bozen.

Head down the road past the bakery (which sells luscious Mohnstrudel – poppy seed pastry). Keep a look-out for the E5 turn-off R (*not* path n.5), threading its way through houses and farms, and dropping to cross the road at the head of Brantental.

Gentle ups and downs follow, to where you join the Forstweg Alte Säge. This is an old pilgrim route that begins with Stations of the Cross and unassuming shrines, and proceeds via a modest cutting. A dip across a stream coincides with a marked geological change, as the wine-red porphyry rock that has accompanied the

Shrine en route to Weißenstein

100

route since Bozen is left behind and lighter sedimentary types take over.

You turn W to climb on a paved way and shortly emerge into a meadow below the buildings of the South Tyrol's most important sanctuary. Turn L into

1hr 30min – Weißenstein/Pietralba (1527m), the name a reference to the pale stone of a nearby mountain. Facilities include a hostel, restaurant and hotel ☎ (39) 0471/615124 **www.pmw.it**, and bus links to Bozen. Do drop in to the Baroque-style church to see the noteworthy collection of *ex votos* (offerings made in fulfilment of a vow). The church's founding legend features a woodcutter who had a healing vision of the Virgin Mary in the course of an illness. However, as he was reputedly 'somewhat simple', nobody believed him, and Our Lady was forced to arrange a reappearance to remind him of his promise of a fitting monument. During the construction of the church a precious alabaster statue was discovered in a grotto, and is now the focus of the sanctuary.

Just before the church a path (E5) climbs L to join a white gravel track (keep L) heading S in woodland full of squirrels. Approximately 45min from the sanctuary, at a junction (Kösertal, 1695m) keep L above the main track, and follow waymarks carefully across a beautiful pasture valley, S for the most part. With continual ups and downs the narrowing path finally reaches the edge of an amazing canyon, where a constantly plunging descent takes you to the valley floor and the head of a waterfall in the wondrous red-tinged

1hr 45min – Butterloch canyon (1554m), also known as Bletterbach, after the river. Starting 15,000 years ago, the stream has excavated to a depth of 400m, to carve out an 8km long course, exposing geological strata ranging from the Permian to the Triassic (280–235 million years ago). A series of giddy but well-anchored ladders (a brief detour off the main E5 route) leads down through geological time – a 2m layer of compressed prehistoric squid for a start, followed by a volcanic

Butterloch canyon

chimney. Numerous fossils, including those of 1000kg herbivorous reptiles, have been unearthed in the vicinity. See **www.bletterbach.info**.

The E5 proceeds straight up the other side of the ravine, through woods brightened with martagon lilies and purple orchids, not to mention awe-inspiring views in both directions. En route are scattered boulders, deposited either by a long-gone glacier or by landslides, though a legend claims otherwise. The story involves Grimm, a giant accused of kidnapping the beautiful daughter of a count from the Ega valley. A battle ensued, with the giant hurling huge rocks onto his pursuers, injuring the men, whose blood flowed into the valley and stained the rocks red. Unfortunately a monstrous landslide then buried both the aggressor and, alas, the luckless maiden.

A bench amid dwarf mountain pine doubles as a lookout onto Weißhorn and its colourful underlying layers. Next, a straightforward stretch, SW across meadows and woods, brings you out at **Zirmerhof** ☎ (39) 0471/887215, **www.zirmerhof.com**, a classy guesthouse with a reputation for hosting writers and thinkers, as well as those who appreciate afternoon tea in style with delicious cakes. **Note** The village of Oberradein/Redagno di sopra, with buses and a geological museum, is accessible via the road near the hotel.

Only minutes downhill is

1hr 30min – Wastlhof (1419m) ☎ (39) 0471/887168. A scenically positioned working farm that offers traditional meals and spotless, old-style lodgings at very reasonable prices.

STAGE 17
Wastlhof to Gfrill

Time	5hr 30min
Distance	19.4km/12 miles
Ascent/Descent	804m/895m
Grade	2
Route profile	see Stage 16
Map	see Stage 16

This a straightforward and averagely interesting day, with lengthy tracts of forest and a moderate number of ups and downs. At the day's end you can collapse into cosy lodgings at Gfrill, where a memorable guesthouse offers brilliant views over the main Verona–Bozen valley, beyond whose patchwork orchards rise the pale, shimmering Brenta Dolomites.

From **Wastlhof** (1419m) the E5/n.9 heads S on an old track that soon becomes a paved path dropping through beech woods. Keep a lookout for markings, as several forks are encountered. A road is crossed, then followed briefly after **Schwarzenbach** hamlet. A forestry track then forks R for the final leg down to

Descent towards Kaltenbrunn

1hr 10min – Kaltenbrunn/Fontanefredde (991m), once renowned for its mineral water springs. Groceries, ATM, bus links to Bozen, and Albergo Fontanefredde ☎ 0471/887022.

Go R along the main road past Albergo Fontanefredde, but soon turn L for the road to Truden. At an information board for Trudnerhorn Nature Park, a signed path breaks off L (SW), then it's uphill through a beautiful if cool conifer forest to join a wider track lined with blackberries and raspberries. This takes you to a saddle on a road, occupied by small but well-placed

50min – Truden/Trodena (1127m). Bus links to Bozen, shops, ① (39) 0471/869078 and visitor centre for the Trudnerhorn Nature Park. There is a scattering of attractive guesthouses, including Gasthof Goldener Adler ☎ (39) 0471/869066.

Follow waymarking n.4 through the village via the church. A short distance below the buildings the E5 branches L to cross a stream. A broad forestry track leads S, traversing forest with impressively tall pine trees, though the occasional glimpse of the distant Adige valley is allowed. The first useful landmark is **Passo Cisa** (1439m, 1hr 20min), where a path goes SSW for a stiff climb, intersecting a track. Higher up the wood has been cleared for pastureland, and this means Dolomite views and

2hr – Hornalm/Malga Corno (1718m). A little below the modest top of Trudnerhorn, this popular family-run restaurant specialises in traditional South Tyrol cuisine, including *Strauben*, delicious soft-fried batter squiggles served hot with redcurrant preserve. Cosy dormitory accommodation, ☎ (39) 330/869959, open 5 May to 31 October, sleeps 9.

A well-signed track continues SSW, uphill through open wood with views over vast swathes of greenery. Paths and track alternate amidst veritable carpets of bilberries, just missing a couple of small lakes. The closing section veers NW, descending on an old sunken pathway to meadows around the tiny hamlet of

The Adige valley seen from Gfrill

1hr 30min – Gfrill/Cauria (1328m). Pension Fichtenhof, ☎ (39) 0471/889028, is a renowned family-run hotel–restaurant with organic vegetables, home-baked bread, delicious jams, *pasta con Teroldego e ragù* (pasta with a local red wine and delicate meat sauce). Phone ahead at peak holiday times. Should the place be fully booked the helpful staff will find you a private room in the vicinity. Stunningly located, the guesthouse overlooks the Adige valley and the narrow Salurn passage, edged by soaring cliffs. Over the centuries the river flooded the Salurn passage repeatedly, causing widespread disruption to transport – see Stage 19 and Dürer.

STAGE 18
Gfrill to Cembra

Time	5hr 45min
Distance	17.2km/10.6 miles
Ascent/Descent	741m/1396m
Grade	1–2
Route profile	see Stage 16

This stage consists mainly of problem-free forest walking. It is a little monotonous at times, but vigilance is essential, as waymarking and useful landmarks are scarce until the lake. This is the final tract in German-speaking territory, as the E5 enters the Trentino region today.

As the stage ends at a rather nondescript town in otherwise picturesque Val di Cembra, consider making the effort to reach Segonzano (Stage 19), a more attractive option. Otherwise, make an overnight stop at lovely Lago Santo, though be aware that the hotel is very popular in midsummer and advance booking essential.

Depart **Gfrill** (1328m) by the *Forstweg* (forestry track) due S in front of the church. ▶ After 1hr there is a huddle of cabins with benches in a clearing at 1475m. Straight afterwards the E5 veers brusquely R, and from here on waymarks are red/white with Italian-only place names.

A narrow path leads through beautiful mixed woods of beech and conifer, and birds of prey may be sighted overhead. A brief down, then the inevitable up, and you emerge on a dirt road with huts at **Passo del Potz Mauer** (1352m, spelt 'Posmar' on maps, 1hr 30min). The E5 turns R again past more huts to descend steadily. After ignoring a path turn-off for Salurn, the route becomes wider and moves closer to the edge of the Adige valley, with splendid views extending to Bozen as well as the Brenta Dolomites.

Walkers are quickly dwarfed by giant pine trees belonging to the Salurner Wald, although the odd clearing affords superb views W to the glaciated Ortler massif.

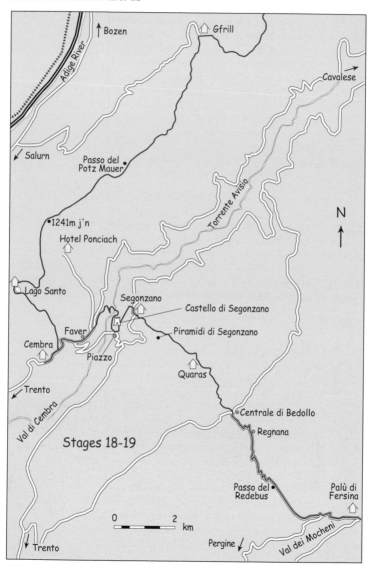

Further on there is a **1241m junction** with a fork L for Hotel Ponciach (☎ 0461/683166). This is a possible short cut, as the route then drops to the Cembra valley at Faver, Stage 19. However, the E5 proceeds S on the 'Sentiero dello Spinello', the name a reference not to illegal substances consumed in cigarette form, but an ancient pathway linking the Adige with the Cembra valley. Along with religious processions, it witnessed the passage of Napoleon's invading troops in the late 1700s.

The pretty path widens and drops past a series of private huts (such as Rifugio Val Zorz), finally coasting along the road to

4hr 30min – Lago Santo (1194m). Albergo Lago Santo, ☎ (39) 0461/683066, sleeps 35, open April to October. Owned by ANA, the Italian Alpine Corps Association, it specialises in hearty meals such as *polenta con funghi* (cornmeal with mushrooms) and meat dishes. (**Note** The building is incorrectly placed on the Kompass map.) The lake itself, a pretty, conifer-lined body of water 210m

Lago Santo

long and 180m wide, but only 15m deep, attracts summer picnickers. The basin was the result of glacial modelling eons ago.

A path circles the lake to its SE end, in common with the Sentiero del Dürer (see introduction to Stage 19). A clear path plunges SE, and as it is paved in parts, it can be slippery when wet. The path cuts across a lane, and soon there are views over the heavily wooded Cembra valley to villages, vineyards, and even the *piramidi* at Segonzano (earth pyramids – see introduction to Stage 19). A concrete ramp leads to the main road at a bus stop. A short stroll R (SW), past the valley's wine-making cooperative premises, brings you to

1hr 15min – Cembra (673m), ① 0461/683110, daily buses to Trento, food shops and Hotel al Caminetto ☎ (39) 0461/683007.

STAGE 19
Cembra to Palù di Fersina

Time	5hr 30min
Distance	17.9km/11.1 miles
Ascent/Descent	920m/200m
Grade	1–2
Map	see Stage 18

Today the E5 follows the beautiful Val di Cembra, with its ruined castle and attractive terraced vineyards, which produce excellent Müller Thurgau white wines, and Schiava, a rosé. Then there are the curious eroded pyramids – *piramidi* – at Segonzano. These demand lengthy exploration, so a good 1hr extra should be allowed.

This walk through the Val di Cembra follows the 'Sentiero del Dürer', which commemorates the route taken by the young German artist Albrecht Dürer. He was travelling down to Venice in 1494–95 to study the great Italian masters, but disastrous flooding in the Adige valley at Salurn obliged him to detour via this alternative route. As it turned out, the detour was something of an advantage, as Dürer made a number of inspired watercolours depicting the castle.

The day's last two hours are along a road – alternatives are hitch-hiking, or calling the Palù di Fersina hotel for a lift if you plan to stay there.

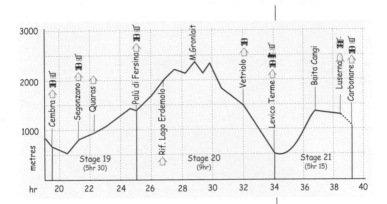

From **Cembra** (673m) follow the main road NE for about 20min to a fork and shrine – keep L and walk through **Faver** (shops, buses to Trento, cafés), which has an unusual number of underground arched passageways. Soon after the fork L to Ponciach (which you ignore), as the buildings start thinning, keep a lookout for the sign R for the lane parallel to the road (NNE). A pretty route through the valley's famed terraced vineyards, it is known as the Via Corvaia, a reference to its many curves, as well as a reminder of the labourers en route to their *corvées*, sessions of hard work in the fields belonging to the lord of the castle that is soon visible ahead.

A rough lane takes over to descend E, past a white-washed shrine dedicated to the Madonna di Pompei and across Torrente Avisio (529m). Turn R below the castle and apple orchards to the hamlet of **Piazzo** (539m). Here

Approaching Segonzano castle

the E5 has been rerouted – fork L up to the ruins of 16th-century **Castello di Segonzano**. The castle was partially destroyed during the invasion by Napoleon's forces in 1796, then further sacked by locals in desperate need of building materials in the aftermath of serious flooding in 1822. If you want, you could treat yourself to a night of luxury at the tastefully restored, sophisticated restaurant–guesthouse Locanda dello Scalco ☎ 0461/696044 **www.locandadelloscalco.it**.

The E5 turns diagonally uphill (NNE), following red marks, through houses and up to the main road and

1hr 45min – Segonzano (816m), or Stedro-Sabion on the map. Regular buses to Trento, groceries, and modern, reasonably priced Hotel alle Piramidi with swimming pool, ☎ (39) 0461/686106 **www.piramidihotel.it**.

Alongside the hotel and the supermarket take the red-waymarked lane L uphill to wind through the pretty village with arched passageways and shrines (keeping well L of the church). At a narrow surfaced road turn L (ESE) through the hamlet of Lech and along to the

30min – Piramidi di Segonzano (900m). There are glimpses of these pyramids from the road, but it's a pity not to admire these curious and quite spectacular sentinels from close range. Knobbly spires in many cases, they are relics of glacial moraine deposited around 50 million years ago and exposed by streams and rainwater. Several different levels have viewing platforms. The base rock here is porphyry once again, while the overlying terrain, 40m deep in parts, is composed of clay, sand and pebbles mixed with chunks of limestone and metamorphic stones, which form the caps of the pyramids. Return to the same point on the road to resume the E5.

The little-used road leads SE to the tiny hamlet of **Quaras** (955m), where Signora Andreatta ☎ 0461/686411 rents out rooms (sleeps 8) and provides simple meals.

Now a lovely old path heads off through abandoned terraces and wooded mountainsides. After a stream in

Earth pyramids at Segonzano

Val Brutta, a cluster of houses (Marteri) is touched on, then it's down to the crossroads at

1hr 15min – Centrale di Bedollo (1078m), groceries, pizzeria, buses to Trento.

Turn R and cut up to the road that climbs via Regnana (1215m) to **Passo del Redebus** (1444m, 1hr 20min) and its restaurant. Stick to the road for the last leg into the Val dei Mocheni and

2hr – Palù di Fersina (1400m). Tiny grocery shop, buses to Pergine and Trento. Albergo Lagorai ☎ (39) 0461/550079 is a good-value hotel whose helpful owner will pick up guests from Centrale di Bedollo and drive them up to the start of the path for Lago Erdemolo the following day, a saving of 1hr. The valley's tourist office is at Sant'Orsola ① (39) 0461/551440. **Hint** If possible, and if a bed happens to be available (not an easy feat in view of the cantakerous nature of the owners), by all means continue in ascent as far as Lago Erdemolo, as this will give you a head start for the long traverse in Stage 20.

The Val di Fersina is also generally known as the Val dei Mocheni, as it is home to another curious Germanic linguistic variation that is spoken nowhere else – in fact the valley is also called Bersntol just to add to the cartographic confusion. In the Middle Ages (1300–1500s) large numbers of expert miners were encouraged to migrate from Bohemia and Bavaria to work the 100 or so sites dotted up the valley. The newcomers formed a separate group and were better off than the local farmers, as the mines (fluorite, pyrite and malachite) proved to be profitable. However, the mining activity gave rise to numerous problems, starting with widespread devastation of the woods, as timber was essential for the furnaces, and pollution of watercourses. About 1000 inhabitants still profess to speak the language and a local institute is enthusiastically encouraging this.

STAGE 20
Palù di Fersina to Levico Terme

Time	9hr
Distance	24.1km/14.9 miles
Ascent/Descent	1236m/2131m
Grade	3
Route profile	see Stage 19

This is an outstanding if outrageously long stage across the rugged Lagorai mountain range (which is metamorphic in origin). An early start is essential, as is reliably good weather, sun protection, and a copious supply of water and food. Early summer may also mean late-lying snow on the high points. Once you've left Lago Erdemolo be aware that there are no places to shelter until Vetriolo Terme, and few other walkers are likely to be encountered until Cima Fravort. However, the day's walking can be shortened by 2hr and 1000m of descent at the end courtesy of the bus from Vetriolo Terme to Levico Terme, where excellent rail and road connections make Valsugana a convenient place to leave or join the E5. What's more, both are spa resorts, so all manner of restorative treatments can be procured!

In bad weather one alternative is to take the bus to Pergine, and from there to Levico Terme. In addition, the Kompass map shows a low-altitude route from Palù along surfaced forestry ways, rejoining the main route at Valico La Bassa.

From the Municipio building at **Palù di Fersina** (1400m) you need the road E that climbs gradually past houses and small farms to the last hamlet of **Frotten**, where Agritur Scalzerhof ☎ (39) 0461/550074 offers meals and accommodation.

A clear, signed track continues climbing steadily S towards the Grua va Hardömbl **mine** (1700m, 1hr) ☎ (39) 0461/550053, fascinating guided visits in summer. However, a little before the entrance to the mine a path (n.325) forks R to cross Torrente Fersina. A good path climbs across lovely meadows dotted with larch, while ahead are ever-improving views of the Lagorai. A distinctive cirque is entered, with a short detour to

1hr 50min – Rifugio Lago Erdemolo (2006m). ☎ (39) 0461/550077, sleeps 18, open 20 June to 20 September. The deep basin shelters a milky-turquoise lake, at the foot of lofty Cima di Cave and Monte del Lago.

A steady climb SSE leads above the tree line across terrain stained by colourful lichen, not to mention alpenrose. About 40min from the lake you reach **Passo del Lago** (2213m), and gentle, rolling upland used as pasture for sheep and cows, along with views down Valsugana. This is the actual start of the long, exhilarating ridge route.

After an abrupt turn R (SSW) you find yourself following a crest with several narrow, exposed stretches,

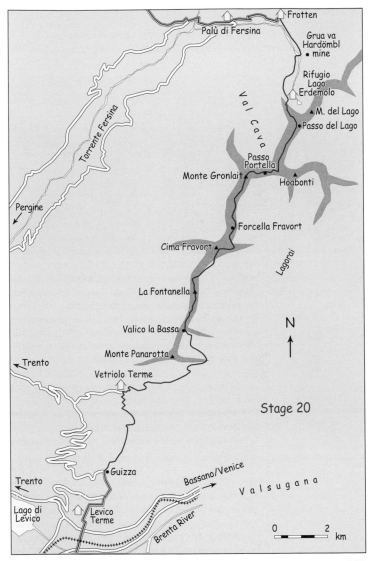

Frotten

Palù di Fersina

Grua va
Hardömbl
• mine

Rifugio
Lago
Erdemolo

▲ M. del Lago

• Passo del Lago

V a l   C a v a

Passo
Portella

Monte Gronlait ▲

Hoabonti ▲

← Pergine

Forcella Fravort •

Cima Fravort ▲

L a g o r a i

La Fontanella ▲

N
↑

Valico la Bassa •

Monte Panarotta ▲

← Trento

Vetriolo Terme

Stage 20

• Guizza

Bassano/Venice →

V a l s u g a n a

← Trento

Lago di
Levico

Levico
Terme

Brenta River

0   2
|————————| km

During the ascent to Monte Gronlait

but this is more than rewarded by stunning panoramas over the Lagorai, including Cima d'Asta E, and W to the Brenta and snowcapped Adamello massifs.

First World War trenches are encountered, then a curious triangular outcrop. Immediately afterwards there is a brief *sentiero alpinistico*, a narrow, cliff-hugging path that requires a sure foot. A short descent via the western flank of triangular Hoabonti brings you to **Passo Portella** (40min, 2152m) at the head of Val Cava (possible escape route).

The going gets a little rough now, as you are required to head W straight up the other side, which is a rubble-ridden shoulder. The climb is punishing, though it eases on the final traverse to the summit cross on

2hr – Monte Gronlait (2383m). Here are breathtaking rewards. The glaciated Carè Alto and Adamello groups spread out W over the Adige valley, flanked by the pale Brenta spires, while a good line up of the Dolomites can be seen NE, not to mention the light-coloured Altopiano di Folgaria-Lavarone S.

First World War trench on Cima Favort

Monte Gronlait seen from Cima Fravort

The clear if narrow path n.325 proceeds along the crest SSW, parallel to the remains of more trenches. Grassy slopes frequented by birds of prey lead down to **Forcella Fravort** (2155m), and an escape route N.

Yet another steep climb is in store, over rubbly red stone, but it is the last of the day. Soon, around the corner, amidst remains of rusty barbed wire, reconstructed First World War trenches and positions are followed en route to the crooked cross on top of

1hr – Cima Fravort (2347m). This amazing vantage point gives an overview of much of the route so far, as well as that to come. The mountain is a popular destination for walkers from Valsugana resorts.

With views to the modest winter ski centre of Panarotta, the E5 embarks on a knee-jarring descent SSW, via modest hillocks such as La Fontanella. Amidst shrubby vegetation, and presided over by impertinent cows, is **Valico la Bassa** (50min, 1834m). The number of sunbathing picnickers here indicates the proximity of civilisation.

The E5 veers S now into fir woods – shade at last! Farm buildings are not far off, though Rifugio Malga

Masi, shown on the map, no longer exists. Turn R along the forestry track and follow its leisurely curves, cutting around Monte Panarotta, moving SW, and down at last to panoramically located

2hr 10min – Vetriolo Terme (1481m). Very popular with hang gliders, who launch themselves from the terrace opposite the bar Maso al Vetriolo Vecchio, ☎ (39) 0461/701564, which has rooms and provides meals. Summertime buses to Levico Terme.

Note Waymarking is decidedly inadequate on this concluding stretch, necessitating extra vigilance.

Turn R along the road for a few minutes to where the E5 forks downhill L (S). A steep, narrow path plunges through woods and crosses a track. A little further down it turns L along Via dei Gòi (near Maso Gòio on the Kompass map), an unsurfaced track bearing briefly W. A series of paths and tracks leads S for the most part, and as the way is generally wooded with no useful landmarks, don't lose sight of the intermittent red/white paint streaks.

After a considerable descent you emerge on tarmac and cross to **Guizza** to take the Strada dei Baroni. From here quiet surfaced roads continue in the same direction to the laid-back spa resort of

2hr – Levico Terme (505m). For the tourist office take a sharp L at the Municipio towards the park and spa. The railway station is a stroll further downhill. ① (39) 0461/706101 or 800/018925. ATM, good range of shops for local produce, such as Crucolo cheese, tasty cold sausages and crisp apples. Restaurants and cafés abound, with outdoor seating where a well-earned glass of Trentino's excellent red Teroldego wine can be enjoyed. Accommodation is plentiful, and rooms can usually be found even at peak times such as mid-August – a mid-range example is Hotel Ideal ☎ (39) 0461/706701, **www.idealevico.it**. There are frequent buses and trains to Trento and Venice; the original stretch of this railway line was laid in 1896 when the region was under Austrian rule. Two inviting lakes, Lago di Levico and Lago di Caldonazzo, are in the vicinity, and campers, windsurfers and boating enthusiasts flock to their shores in summer.

The Valsugana has been a strategic transport artery since at least Roman times, when the Via Claudia Augusta ran along it. It also coincides with a significant fault line, and even the least geologically minded walker cannot fail to notice that it separates the dark metamorphic Lagorai chain from the pale sedimentary plateau of the Altopiano di Folgaria-Lavarone.

STAGE 21
Levico Terme to Carbonare

Time	4hr 30min to Luserna + 45min by bus to Carbonare
Distance	14.4km/8.9 miles (on foot)
Ascent/Descent	865m/50m
Grade	2
Route profile	see Stage 19

The E5 climbs out of the Valsugana today. A stiff ascent up the thickly forested, apparently impenetrable northern flanks of the Altopiano di Folgaria-Lavarone leads to the dramatically placed village of Luserna, yet another 'island' of linguistic importance. Up here reminders of the First World War are plentiful, mainly in the form of sizeable forts. From Luserna there is a bus to Carbonare, not an exceptionally exciting place, and you could consider proceeding to Passo Coe and Stage 22 if time and daylight permit.

To leave **Levico Terme** (505m), continue straight ahead (S) downhill from the Municipio. The fourth turn-off L (Via Prà) cuts diagonally down to the main road and a level crossing. (From the railway station go W for 5min to

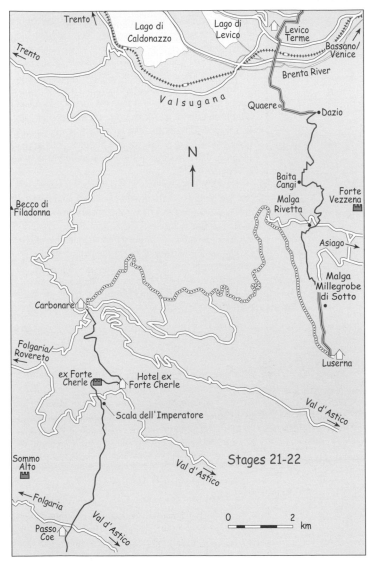

Trento

Lago di
Caldonazzo

Lago di
Levico

Levico
Terme

Bassano/
Venice

Trento

Brenta River

Valsugana

Quaere

Dazio

N

Becco di
Filadonna

Baita
Cangi

Forte
Vezzena

Malga
Rivetta

Asiago

Malga
Millegrobe
di Sotto

Carbonare

Folgaria/
Rovereto

Luserna

ex Forte
Cherle

Hotel ex
Forte Cherle

Scala dell'Imperatore

Val d'Astico

Sommo
Alto

Stages 21-22

Val d'Astico

Folgaria

0   2 km

Passo
Coe

Val d'Astico

reach this point). Shortly, a major road and the Brenta river are crossed. Not long after, take the road branching L (SSE), with a red/white marking and E5 on a telegraph pole. The route goes through fields of Indian corn and orchards of apples to the hamlet of **Quaere**.

Take a L turn past sprinkler-watered crops. You curve L past a church and go R at the next junction for **Dazio** (499m), an ancient customs point on the strategic, formerly paved communications route between Levico and the Altipiano. Here at last you are pointed R off the road for path n.201, and curiously named Valle Pisciavacca ('cow pee'!).

The climb that follows is through mixed woods with plenty of orchids, gentians and cyclamen, and bleached white rock. A couple of minor streams are crossed, while clearings allow wonderful views back to Levico and its twin lakes. A shrine is followed by a short, helpful stretch of chain, as the terrain here is somewhat crumbly. You soon emerge at

The twin lakes in Valsugana near Levico Terme

2hr 45min – Baita Cangi (1370m), a tiny private hut in Spiazzo della Volpe ('the fox's clearing'). Turn L (E) along

the old First World War military road, past rock faces pitted with man-made caverns. Some 20min on, immediately after a gate, don't miss the turn-off R (S) leading through to the road. (A brief detour R brings you to popular snack bar–restaurant **Malga Rivetta**, while Forte Vezzena is a short distance E.)

Straight up the other side you pass a ski lift and soon join a lane. At a second lift go sharp L to cross the piste and join a lovely track through woodland. Further on at a major junction you need to turn L. A gentle uphill stretch brings you out on a road which is followed R downhill past the summer restaurant Malga Millegrobe di sotto. Amazing views onto the jagged green mountains of the Pasubio range, also known as the Piccole Dolomiti, accompany you into the pleasant village of

1hr 45min – Luserna (1319m), set dramatically on a precipitous cliff edge overlooking the deep cleft of Val d'Astico. Controversy surrounds the origin of this place name: some claim it derives from Celtic 'liz', commonly used across the Alps for 'pasture', while others prefer the local explanation, which is from 'shine', a reference to either sun reflected on rooftops or the glow of the fires of the charcoal burners. ATM, groceries. ① 0464/789638, and museum illustrating turn-of-the-century life in this curious 'linguistic island' of Cimbro. Closest accommodation to the square is Agritur Galeno ☎ (39) 0464/789723, **www.agriturgaleno.com**, or the modest hotel Lusernarhof ☎ (39) 0464/788010, **www.lusernarhof.it**, at Tezze, just below the main village.

A 45min bus trip brings you to **Carbonare (1074m)**, dominated to the NW by impressive Becco di Filadonna. ① (39) 0464/765377. Sleep and eat at friendly Albergo Cornetto ☎ 0464/765131, or another of the sprinkling of hotels. There are regular bus links to Trento and Rovereto. A supermarket sells local produce such as tasty Vezzena or Asiago cheese, and bear in mind that these are the last groceries you'll be able to purchase until Giazza, Stage 26.

STAGE 22
Carbonare to Passo Coe

Time	3hr
Distance	9.5km/5.9 miles
Ascent/Descent	626m/90m
Grade	2
Map	see Stage 21

A leisurely stage that can either be tacked on to Stage 21, or enjoyed as a semi-rest day in view of the long traverse that comes afterwards. Birdwatchers will have a field day on the open pastureland, while flower enthusiasts will not be disappointed, especially in the summer months. A decent hotel–restaurant is encountered en route, but the day's highlight is a labyrinthine fort (a torch is useful for exploring).

Forte Cherle dates back to the First World War, when the southernmost confine of the extensive but slowly decaying Austro–Hungarian Empire still cut across the Altopiano. In 1907, with the prospect of military conflict with Italy looming, the Austrians began constructing a massive system of seven forts linked by trenches and fortifications, and supplied by mechanised cableways from the Valsugana and Val Lagarina (Rovereto). The Italians did likewise, connecting to the adjoining Asiago plateau to the E, though on a lesser scale. The first shot was reportedly fired in the early morning of 24 May 1915, heralding long years of devastation. All the inhabitants of the northernmost villages were hurriedly evacuated to faraway camps in Bohemia (now the Czech Republic), to be housed as refugees in *Barakenlager*, clusters of draughty wooden huts. Not everyone returned.

From the church at **Carbonare** (1074m) head up the road for Folgaria. Only minutes along, at a fountain and shrine (signpost), branch L (S). Not far on fork L again for a lane through pretty beech woods and past fascinating reddish rock formations embedded with fossils. A clear-

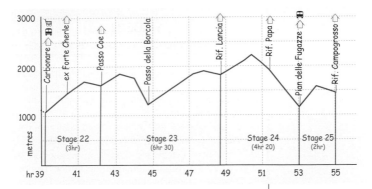

ing houses Malga Clama (1256m). Not far uphill is the road and **Hotel ex Forte Cherle** (1436m, ☎ 0464/765103), with lovely views.

Turn R (WNW) across thick spreads of carline thistles to

1hr 10min – ex Forte Cherle (1445m). Dating back to 1909–13, the fort's underground tunnels and Howitzer

Exploring Forte Cherle

positions are ruined but explorable. The 2.5m reinforced concrete roofing was largely removed in 1936 so that iron desperately needed by Italy could be extracted from it. The shortage of iron was caused by an embargo imposed on the fascists as a result of their invasion of Ethiopia. The remaining walls of the fort are extensively pitted by grenades, and bomb craters are still visible in the surrounding area.

A lane leads SE and across a road near a military cemetery. Opposite, the E5 ascends the so-called 'Scala dell'Imperatore' ('emperor's staircase'), supposedly constructed for the visit of the heir-to-the-throne. Dubbed the Staircase of Death by soldiers, it consists of 185 stone steps up to the site of an Austrian wartime hospital, a poignant spot in peaceful pine woods.

Continuing S, thick woods and clearings where raspberries grow are common. A track is crossed close to summer farms, and a bare 1700m hill gained. The hill is extensively scarred with craters and the remains of trenches, which testify to its former proximity to the front line. It also gives huge views over the rolling pasture-lands of the plateau, and WNW is a glimpse of another imposing fort, Sommo Alto.

Heading SW the path descends steeply via a rocky flank to thickly flowered meadows frequented by birds of prey. ◄ Over a rise is the day's destination, and beyond it, due S, Monte Maggio, visited tomorrow.

The occasional depressions are sinkholes, as this terrain is karstic – a limestone base eroded by rainwater.

1hr 50min – Passo Coe (1610m). Rifugio La Stua ☎ (39) 0464/720410, sleeps 22 in comfortable rooms. They serve generous multi-course meals of *orzetto*, a hearty barley soup, *goulasch* with *polenta*, and *castagne con miele*, chestnuts with honey. *Tabiel della casa* is worth trying – a platter of local cheeses and cold sausages. Across the road and under the same management is newly renovated Rifugio Coe ☎ (39) 0464/721754, sleeps 20 in small dorms. Botany enthusiasts may be interested in the Giardino Botanico Alpino, 15min W down the road.

STAGE 23
Passo Coe to Rifugio Lancia

Time	6hr 30min
Distance	15.7km/9.7 miles
Ascent/Descent	939m/724m
Grade	2
Route profile	see Stage 22

A wonderful, solitary stage that rates among the best on the E5, with marvellous wide-reaching views – hopefully with none of the drifting mist that afflicts this region. In fact it is inadvisable to embark on this stage in adverse weather conditions, such as fog, because orientation becomes problematic. Animal life is plentiful, in the shape of chamois, song birds and birds of prey. In all, the day is pretty tiring because of the distance covered, and continual hefty ups and downs. Take plenty of food and drinking water – although several springs are found en route, they should not be relied on.

Note The latter part of this stage, together with the start of Stage 24, takes a long detour loop across pretty upland, touching on well-placed Rifugio Lancia before traversing the dramatic rocky points of the Pasubio. It is possible, though a great pity, to shorten the route by cutting S at the signed junctions either near Malga Costa or at the Sorgente, and heading straight for Rifugio Papa.

Alongside Rifugio La Stua at **Passo Coe** (1610m) the E5 strikes out S across the Alpi di Zonta as broad path n.124. ▶ Soon in conifer woods popular with mushroom gatherers, watch out for red/white waymarks veering L (E) through muddy stretches around the base of a hill. Half an hour from Passo Coe an old military road is gained – turn R (S) for the gentle climb to the cross on

The undulating karstic terrain is thickly grassed and provides important pasture in this cheese-producing region.

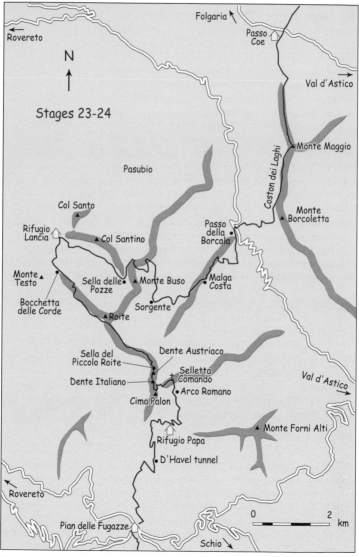

Stages 23-24

Folgaria

Rovereto

Passo Coe

Val d'Astico

N

Pasubio

Monte Maggio

Coston dei Laghi

Col Santo

Rifugio Lancia

Col Santino

Passo della Borcola

Monte Borcoletta

Monte Testo

Bocchetta delle Corde

Sella delle Pozze

Monte Buso

Malga Costa

Sorgente

Roite

Sella del Piccolo Roite

Dente Austriaco

Selletta Comando

Val d'Astico

Dente Italiano

Arco Romano

Cima Palon

Monte Forni Alti

Rifugio Papa

D'Havel tunnel

Rovereto

0   2 km

Pian delle Fugazze

Schio

1hr – Monte Maggio (1853m). The vast views from here even take in the Brenta Dolomites NW. Spring 1916 saw a three-day offensive by Austrian forces across the Altopiano di Folgaria-Lavarone. It included the occupation of Monte Maggio and its fort, a disastrous episode for the Italians, as this was one of their key positions. A good part of the Altopiano remained in Austrian hands until the end of the First World War.

Continuing S on the L side of the rocky crest called Coston dei Laghi, the path becomes somewhat narrower and on a level. ▶ In places you follow averagely exposed rock ledges, and man-made caverns are numerous. It's a beautiful route, high above rugged, densely wooded valleys plunging off the central ridge, and the wide-ranging views soon include the Sogli Bianchi outcrop, to be crossed in the forthcoming section.

Once the prominent rocky point **Monte Borcoletta** (1759m) is rounded, the path begins its sharp descent in tight zigzags through beech woods. An abandoned marble quarry is passed, as is a derelict house with its own

Very little evidence of other human beings is evident. Dwarf mountain pine grows thickly here, and is a favourite haunt of chamois.

Nearing Monte Borcoletta, view to Sogli Bianchi

vintage truck, well into the advanced stages of rusting. Then it's not far to the quiet pass on the road at

1hr 30min – Passo della Borcola (1207m). A short distance downhill R a farm offers modest meals and refreshments (midsummer only). There is no public transport. History enthusiasts may like to stroll briefly L (S) to see the stone plaque, complete with winged lion, dating back to 1472 and marking the former border between the Republic of Venice and Trento.

The E5 proceeds as n.147 – straight up the other side of the road. Initially due S, it climbs into light woods and passes a spring marked by a plaque, courtesy of Austrian soldiers in 1916. It's a steady winding climb, essentially SW, up into a vast rocky pasture basin where more dwarf mountain pine flourish. The 1740m mark means another spring, indicated by the sign *acqua* ('water'). Not much further up a clear line of war-time trenches stands out, and high over the Sogli Bianchi the land levels out with scattered remains of tunnels and buildings.

After the ruins of landmark **Malga Costa** (1830m), now the haunt of huge ravens, low marker poles show

The path passes Bisorte

the way across a grassy plateau to a junction (a variant breaks off to Zenevri, from where you can reach Rifugio Papa) where the main route bears R. Heading W, the path drops across scree and through light woods to a flight of stone steps and another spring, **Sorgente**, not shown on the Kompass map (1845m, 2hr 30min to here). Here, too, a direct route for Rifugio Papa forks off S.

From here onwards old military roads ensure leisurely walking and good views. Heading N at first, you cut the eastern flank of Monte Buso to a saddle alongside the elongated crest of Bisorte. After a brief drop S a track is joined where you turn L for the broad saddle

3hr 20min – Sella delle Pozze (1903m). Path n.102 breaks off S here, a medium-altitude variant to Selletta Commando in Stage 24.

This last leg involves a leisurely trek NW across undulating karstic upland, colonised by alpenrose shrubs and larch, and bounded by Col Santino R (N) and the northern outliers of the Pasubio S.

Rifugio Lancia

After the modest summer farm Malga Pozze, the track drops into a lovely pasture basin at the foot of the renowned lookout Col Santo. **Note** In view of the undrinkable water at Rifugio Lancia, it's a good idea to fill bottles at the spring (*sorgente*) that precedes your arrival at this excellent establishment.

40min – Rifugio Lancia (1825m) ☎ (39) 0464/868068 SAT, sleeps 64, open June to September then weekends May and October. Cosy refuge that feeds its guests well. It may seem incongruous, but yes, the Lancia of the refuge was the same figure as the automobile entrepreneur. In the 1930s plans were underway to develop this zone into a ski resort linked with Rovereto. Fortunately, after a single ski lift was dismantled due to the difficulty of maintaining an access road snow-free, these plans came to nothing. The refuge itself was completed in 1939.

STAGE 24
Rifugio Lancia to Pian delle Fugazze

Time	4hr 20min
Distance	14.7km/9.1 miles
Ascent/Descent	395m/1058m
Grade	2
Route profile	see Stage 22
Map	see Stage 23

One of the most interesting if sobering stages on the E5, today leads across the Pasubio crests, arena of devastation and shocking loss of life during the First World War – the figure for casualties is estimated at 38,000. In May 1916 the troops of the Austrian Empire set out to occupy the Altipoano di Folgaria and the Pasubio, with the intention of subsequently moving down into the Po plain and attacking the

Italian forces that were lined up along the Isonzo river (now in Slovenia).

Under Italian General Achille Papa the advance was brought to a halt on the highest ridges of the Pasubio range. However, for two long years both sides dug in, and the mountains are honeycombed with tunnels, positions and supply roads, and scarred by mine damage. Italy's fascist regime declared the zone 'sacred to the fatherland' in the 1920s, and transformed it into a protected area – with questionable additions such as a mock Roman arch! Despite this, visitors unfailingly leave with an awareness of senseless tragedy.

After Rifugio Papa the E5 follows a military road, named 'Strada degli Eroi' ('road of the heroes') under Mussolini to commemorate the fallen. Snaking its 6km way down a sheer mountain face, through 2.3km of rock-hewn tunnels, it is a triumph of civil engineering. It ends at a strategic road pass, Pian delle Fugazze, with transport and accommodation, so a good place to stop over. However, if possible do press on for the further 2hr of Stage 25 to Rifugio Campogrosso, as this will see you well placed for the long traverse that follows.

Note In bad weather, to avoid the high ridges exposed to the elements, it is advisable to return to Sella delle Pozze in Stage 23 and follow n.120 over lower-lying land to Selletta Commando – 2hr from Rifugio Lancia.

From **Rifugio Lancia** (1825m) head due S on n.102, past masses of rock thick with fossilised shells, and into larch woods. The first landmark is **Bocchetta delle Corde** (1894m), close to modest Monte Testo. Ignore the pointers branching off for Val di Foxi and proceed steadily SE on n.105 through dwarf mountain pines. With impressive views W over the Adige valley to Carè Alto and the Brenta Dolomites, the path moves briefly to the R (SW) side of the main Pasubio ridge, accompanied by lines of trenches dominating a wild, scree-spattered valley. It climbs imperceptibly through hardy shrubs and flowers, such as thrift and mountain avens, before reaching path junction

1hr 20min – Sella del Piccolo Roite (2111m), above a former Austrian encampment.

On the Dente Austriaco

A sharp R sees you ascending through chaotic rubble, trenches and all manner of debris to the commanding position of the **Dente Austriaco** (Austrian Tooth, 2127m), with its modest altar, flagpoles, and wooden cross adorned with barbed wire. The path crosses this desolate, castle-like formation to its far southern corner, marked by a concrete fort and machine gun positions.

The path drops quickly to a 2180m saddle. Straight ahead are unbelievably chaotic stone blocks strewn down the mountain flank – the outcome of exploded mines. Path n.105 climbs over what's left of the **Dente Italiano** (2220m), riddled by an underground tunnel network. Down at the far end is **Selletta Damaggio** (2175m) at the foot of Cima Palon. Here broad path n.142 leads L (E) to descend across a desert-like landscape to

50min – Selletta Comando (2075), and Chiesetta di Santa Maria. A monument also honours the memory of partisans who lost their lives during the closing years of the Second World War. Alpine choughs are apparently the only form of life in the area. Here the direct variant routes join up.

An unsurfaced road heads S now, past the so-called Arco Romano and down through desolate terrain to the helicopter pad at **Porte del Pasubio** (gateways to the Pasubio). The high ridge stretching westwards with Monti Forni Alti is the site of the renowned 'Strada delle Gallerie', a road hewn through the mountain with 51 tunnels totalling over 6.5km, and well worth exploring if time allows.

The Dente Italiano pitted with wartime caverns

Just around the corner R, in a stunningly scenic position is

30min – Rifugio Papa (1928m) ☎ (39) 0445/630233 CAI, sleeps 40, open June to September then weekends. The refuge was not named after a leading religious figure, but after General Achille Papa.

The E5 now embarks on the 'Strada degli Eroi', an unsurfaced road that is closed to motorised traffic, but popular with mountain bikers. It winds its exciting way S around sharp, exposed corners and through countless tunnels. At the 1780m mark the D'Havel tunnel cuts through to moderately gentler slopes. Now there are

Rifugio Papa

numerous path short cuts, steep at times, and on loose stones, hard going for knees and ankles. Once in beech woods don't be tempted by the path marked for Streva, but stick to the main track for the final stretch down to

1hr 40min – Pian delle Fugazze (1162m). Modern Locanda al Passo ☎ (39) 0464/89135. Year-round buses to Rovereto as well as a summer service via Schio (trains) to Vicenza.

Mist on the Strada degli Eroi

STAGE 25
Pian delle Fugazze to Rifugio Campogrosso

Time	2hr
Distance	4.8km/2.9 miles
Ascent/Descent	423m/128m
Grade	2
Route profile	see Stage 22

This short stage is virtually a rest day – unless you tack it on to the end of Stage 24. It traverses the interesting if minor Sengio Alto group in the heart of the Piccole Dolomiti. The destination is a very pleasant refuge-cum-guesthouse that does delicious meals. An even easier alternative takes the quiet 6km road, closed to traffic, skirting Sengio Alto.

From the road pass at **Pian delle Fugazze** (1162m) follow the road SW for Campogrosso. Only minutes along, the E5/n.170 breaks off L, heading diagonally towards a defunct ski lift. You need to hunt around for waymarks at first, but once an old house is gained, both the path and paint splashes reappear. Now it's a steady zigzag S through a beautiful beech wood and across a cascading stream.

A little over 1hr from the road is **Selletta Nord-ovest** (1585m), on the western flank of Monte Cornetto. Continue in the same direction, via a curious rock ledge that affords great views ahead to the Carega group.

The path descends quickly over scree, detouring a farm (Malga Boffetal), and turns L across pasture to a pond. A lane is crossed, then there is a slight climb over a rise below the imposing Sengio Alto chain, beloved of rock climbers. A good path takes the last leg through woods and drops to the road for welcoming

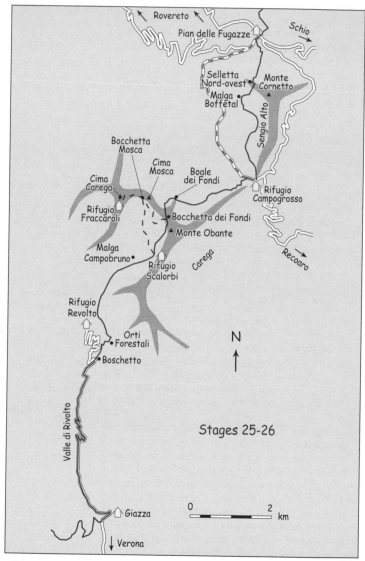

Stages 25-26

2hr – Rifugio Campogrosso (1457m) ☎ (39) 0445/75030, open April to mid-October, then weekends only. Sleeps 60 in dorms and private rooms. A great place to stay overnight, this well-run refuge is frequented by climbers. The building faces the north face of the Carega group, traversed by the E5 tomorrow. Summer bus via Recoaro to Vicenza.

STAGE 26
Rifugio Campogrosso to Giazza

Time	4hr 45min
Distance	16km/9.9 miles
Ascent/Descent	583m/1281m
Grade	2–3

The E5's final stage of Alpine landscapes, this is a very exciting day's walking, with the traverse of the Carega massif ('armchair' in Veneto dialect), and an optional, straightforward summit loop. Good weather is essential for navigation and because of the occasional difficulty of the terrain. There are several refuges along the way, which are useful for an in-depth exploration of this beautiful group of mountains, but early/late season visitors are advised to phone ahead to check opening times. Later on, the route descends a long, steep-sided valley to the first of the sleepy villages in the low-altitude Monti Lessini.

Only minutes W along the road from **Rifugio Campogrosso** (1457m) the E5/n.157 breaks off L for a gentle climb SW through woods. A wide rock neck soon gives wonderful views onto the Carega and Sengio Alto. Now in pure Dolomite terrain, i.e. blinding white rock and scree, soaring peaks, dwarf mountain pines and alpenrose, you traverse W in a gradual ascent in the direction of an isolated tower, Sojo dei Cotorni.

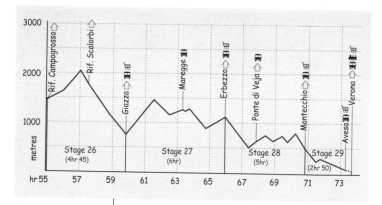

The jagged profile of Cima Mosca ('fly') looms W, while straight ahead is a vast rock-wall barrier at the head of an amphitheatre.

About 1hr from the road, turn L at the **Boale dei Fondi** fork (1632m). Next is a stiff climb SW up a vast rubble gully where several short stretches require a hands-on clamber. ◄ Close to the top, the path veers L and across loose scree, then rock steps lead to a narrow cleft below Monte Obante.

2hr – Bocchetta dei Fondi (2040m), and remarkable contrasts. The NE flanks just ascended are dramatic and rugged, whereas the SW side you now look down over is gentler, grassy and undulating.

Note A signed path aided by a fixed chain breaks off R (NW) for Rifugio Fraccaroli – for experienced walkers only. A more straightforward route is explained in the 'loop' below.

In a matter of minutes the E5 drops L to a nearby junction.

Loop via Cima Carega (2hr)

If the weather warrants it, instead of heading downhill for Rifugio Scalorbi, turn sharp R (NW) on a scenic path high over a spectacular amphitheatre. It transits via **Bocchetta Mosca** (2029m, 15min) before embarking on a straightforward climb in wide curves to modest Rifugio

Cima Carega and Bocchetta Mosca

Fraccaroli ☎ (39) 045/7050033, CAI, sleeps 25, open late June to mid-September. From here you can reach **Cima Carega** 2259m. On a good day views range as far as Lake Garda and even the Adriatic, without forgetting the Dolomites. Afterwards return to Bocchetta Mosca and take the clear path down the middle of the valley to Rifugio Scalorbi.

You plunge downhill S towards the refuge, visible in the grassy basin below. Keep an eye out for the sketchy waymarks.

30min – Rifugio Scalorbi (1767m) ☎ (39) 045/7847029, sleeps 20, open 20 June to 20 September. The adjacent chapel is always open for emergency shelter. Close at hand is a curiously named saddle, Passo Pelagatta ('skin a cat'), presumably a reference to the infamous legend that the natives of Vicenza are in the habit of eating cats! The loop route via Cima Carega rejoins the main route here.

Note In bad weather avoid the following path, as it is subject to rock falls and has narrow, slippery stretches, and take the dirt road instead.

A marked path drops WSW close to Malga Campobruno (1667m), over mountainsides honey-combed with marmot burrows. Soon the valley narrows unexpectedly, as does the path, clinging to the rock flank dizzily high above a stream. A dramatic gorge with sheer walls is close by, and short pieces of chain aid walkers along exposed tracts that could be slippery in the wet.

A good 45min down, a fork leads off R to nearby Rifugio Revolto (☎ 045/7847039, sleeps 25, open mid-summer and weekends), whereas the E5 continues S on Sentiero degli Orti, in a forestry reserve of mostly beech woods. Marked junction **Orti Forestali** (1217m) is fol-lowed by a zigzag to cross the Progno d'Illasi stream, then immediately turn L. Follow the red/white splashes carefully and you should soon emerge on a quiet road at a cluster of houses, called Boschetto (1151m), in the Valle di Rivolto. From here on you follow the tarmac road S the rest of the way (1hr), with the odd short cut, down the beautiful wooded valley, past peaceful hamlets and photogenic haystacks, to the simple village of

2hr 15min – Giazza (759m), from the Latin for 'ice', and also known as Ljetzan in ancient Cimbro. As early as the 1300s ice was an important industry in the Illasi valley. Up until the 1950s, when refrigerators reached the region, slabs would be cut in winter months and stored in semi-underground huts to be transported at night to the homes of the Veronese nobility.

Hotel Belvedere ☎ (39) 045/7847020, is a modest, family-run establishment, open all year except November. Daily buses to Verona. Basic groceries, pizzeria, and folk museum dedicated to the Cimbro lan-guage and culture, which are undergoing a revival here – it's reportedly 'cool' for kids to speak Cimbro nowadays.

STAGE 27
Giazza to Erbezzo

Time	6hr
Distance	19.7km/12.2 miles
Ascent/Descent	1101m/742m
Grade	1–2
Route profile	see Stage 26

With the high mountains well behind it now, the E5 spends its concluding three days exploring the lovely Monti Lessini, with a wealth of landscapes and cultural and natural marvels in store. This stage is relatively low altitude all day, but there are plenty of ups and downs in store in the Monti Lessini Regional Park.

The landscape undergoes a surprising change – it is dominated by rolling hills dotted with outcrops of white limestone, in addition to the attractive red *rosso ammonitico* rock, studded with sizeable fossils left by the coiled, chambered nautilus mollusc, amongst others. This attractive stone has been quarried for centuries to pave the cities of the Veneto. Locally, upright slabs act as field dividers, fencing, and even as long-lasting roofing tiles for traditional rural buildings, though heaving them onto the rafters requires considerable strength!

The rich pastures of the Monti Lessini mean that this is also an important dairy sector, producing flavoursome cheeses. On the practical side, grazing cows are constant companions and walkers should be sure to close gates after them. The open grasslands are also perfect hunting grounds for a range of birds of prey, such as the red kite.

Note The hotels in this district tend to close without warning at the end of the summer season, or during prolonged periods of poor weather, so always phone ahead to check that your choice of accommodation is available.

From the upper part of **Giazza** (759m) and the hotel, cut down through the village to the main square, with its

church and modest museum. On the corner of a bar–restaurant the E5 takes a winding paved path down past neat houses to cross the torrent. It now embarks on a 700m climb, rendered virtually effortless by the easy curves of a perfectly graded old track westward into the realms of the Lessini Park. En route through hazel and beech woods there are cyclamens in flower and tidy piles of chopped firewood, not to mention a short tunnel.

The track eventually emerges from the woods onto bare rolling pastureland, dotted with tiny farms and pale limestone outcrops, landscape typical of the Monti Lessini. On a broad crest you meet up with a lane (1469m, 1hr 45min), near Pampari on the Kompass map. Turn L here towards a farm, but keep a lookout for an abrupt turn-off R (N), downhill across fields. A curious red stone outcrop is encountered and a surfaced road soon afterwards. A matter of minutes along R are stretches of slab fencing, and an attractive stone building, referred to as **ex Osteria Spiazzoi**.

Follow red/white waymarks with special care from here on, as the terrain is criss-crossed with confusing tracks left by cows, mushroom hunters and woodcutters. Due W, the E5 drops through beech woods and dips across a desolate pasture valley. Up the other side, it reaches a characteristic cluster of stone-roofed houses, the hamlet of **Merli** (1256m).

A wide dirt track is followed SW past a church (Santa Anna), before bearing N past more rural buildings, lovely constructions despite the place name, Brutti ('ugly'!). It's not far to a minor road at

3hr 30min – Maregge (1264m), local restaurant Locanda Maregge, church, Verona bus (summer weekends only).

Turn R along the road for the start of a path heading W over a rise. A double row of stone slabs then leads down into a pretty pasture valley to a beautiful cluster of restored stone houses at Tinazzo. Via a lovely lane is a further hamlet, **Zamberlini** (1234m), a sizeable place that boasts a well.

After a distinctive rock cleft and a modest wooded rise, you reach a chapel and join a farm lane. Going S now, there is a working dairy farm at Scala. A narrow, surfaced farm road leads out of the basin to recommended restaurant and hotel **Albergo Croce** (1147m, ☎ (39) 045/7050042).

Opposite the hotel a clear path continues W past Lesi, gradually descending into the gloomy Vaio dell'Anguilla ('valley of the eel'). After an interminably long stretch S amidst damp undergrowth, the E5 makes up its mind to branch R for a surprisingly steep climb W. It's not far now up to the main road and

Hamlet of Merli

2hr 30min – Erbezzo (1118m). Modernish village with ATM, groceries, year-round bus to Verona. Albergo Berna ☎ (39) 045/7075018. 5min down the road is bed and breakfast at Bar Ristorante al Terrazzo ☎ (39) 045/7075023. Otherwise, an excellent fallback is a spotless room at friendly Bar Ristorante Campedelli ☎ (39) 045/7075012, 4.2km away at Cappella Fasani – they provide a free taxi service, and return you to the same place the following morning.

STAGE 28
Erbezzo to Montecchio

Time	5hr
Distance	20km/12.4 miles
Ascent/Descent	450m/1072m
Grade	2
Route profile	see Stage 26
Map	see Stage 27

Today the E5 follows the Valpantena, parallel to the more famous Valpolicella, 'valley of the many blessings', which include wine! Needless to say, memorable bottles are available at restaurants along the way. This stage's highlight is the soaring natural rock bridge, Ponte di Veja, a spectacular sight. The only blight is the inordinate amount of tarmac later on, but there are several villages with bus services en route, should you be tempted. A series of constant ups and downs makes for a tiring day, though some walkers will want to press on with Stage 29 to Verona itself.

Note Walkers must keep a constant eye out for red/white E5 way-markings, as a host of lanes and tracks are encountered.

Close to the main square at **Erbezzo** (1118m) a marked path cuts through houses, leading S to a wooded ridge high over the Vaio dell'Anguilla. It touches briefly on the

Ponte di Veja

road at several points. At the scatter of houses that go by the name of Portello, the route veers R (W), soon reaching **La Rocca** (bus stop for Verona), a wonderful lookout point for the natural rock bridge Ponte di Vejo.

Straight across the road alongside a house the E5 embarks on an overgrown path dropping into the thickly wooded, minor Marcuora valley. At the bottom (400m) turn R along a surfaced road until a clear path breaks off L. You soon find yourself in a beautiful side valley, with cascading streams, and a host of exotic ferns and jungle-like vegetation growing upwards beneath soaring limestone cliffs to the amazing natural arch. ▶ The path climbs to the top of the bridge, and turning R, to the roadside and

At the foot of the arch is a spring and a cave, Grotta dell' Orso ('bear cave'), once home to prehistoric man, since succeeded by a colony of bats.

2hr – Ponte di Veja (620m) (pronounced 'veya'). Hotel Ponte di Veja ☎ (39) 045/7545048. Bus to Verona.

Turn L (E) along the road, lined with chestnut trees, to a lane where the E5 resumes R (S) via a lane. This is a lovely scenic stretch, with glimpses of the quarries that represent work for so many of the region's inhabitants.

You're soon back on the road into **Giare** (684m, bus to Verona), continuing past houses and quarries to an intersection, recognisable by **Ristorante Da Lara** and a shop with local products, including bread and cheeses.

The E5 keeps L on a minor lane for 15min through horse-riding establishments, before joining a road to reach a junction and shrine (**Cappella Fiamene**). Turn R here, downhill past the village of Saline. Take care not to miss the branch 5min on, amidst terracing, for a concrete ramp L gradually ascending into wood. ◀ There is soon more tarmac, the odd short cut, and immediately after Case Antolini, veer L for the hamlet of Dondolo. A path through oak and chestnut traverses modest Monte Tondo (704m), with unusual black basalt rocks underfoot, reminders of ancient volcanic activity. A lane descends easily S to the quiet village of

Views range wide over the surrounding countryside as you cross Monte Comune, with even a glimpse of the southern part of Lake Garda.

3hr – Montecchio (495m), with a handful of traditional restaurants, and a bed and breakfast with cooking facilities courtesy of E5 pioneers Franco and Helene Cuoghi, Via Don Tacchella 21 ☎ (39) 045/6015013. Very occasional bus to Verona.

STAGE 29
Montecchio to Verona

Time	2hr 30min to Avesa + 20min by bus to Verona
Distance	7.3km/4.5 miles (on foot)
Ascent/Descent	50m/448m
Grade	2–3
Route profile	see Stage 26
Map	see Stage 27

This concluding stage explores a deep, dark canyon overgrown with jungle-like vines and creepers. Dominated by towering walls, and only

20m across at its widest point, it is beset with minor landslips and fallen trees, which can make the going pretty tiring. The E5 finally emerges in a pretty farming valley thick with flourishing grape vines – quite a conclusion to this epic trek. Walkers then catch the local bus into the heart of wonderful Verona, a fitting reward!

Note Under no circumstances should walkers head out on this section in anything but perfect weather, as the ladders are exposed and possible rock falls could be extremely dangerous. Even in normal conditions the valley route is muddy, slippery and tiring. The straightforward alternative is to follow the quiet road E out of Montecchio, taking the first branch R (S) for Avesa.

At **Montecchio** (495m) you need the road between the church and Trattoria Il Solito Posto. The E5 soon branches L, making its way W across a field. It dips quickly in and out of a damp valley through mixed wood, featuring spiky butcher's broom. ▶ Not far along, following a brief climb, is the beginning of a succession of steep, airy, metal ladders, firmly attached to the cliffside to aid descent.

Take care when on the downhill sections, as the clay terrain is inevitably slippery.

Ladders in the Borago valley

A natural ledge under an overhang comes halfway, and eventually you find yourself on the dank (if not a little creepy) floor of the Borago valley, dwarfed by increasingly steep rock flanks dripping with creepers. Although waymarks are few and far between, wayfinding is not a problem, as the E5 heads due S, sticking to the trickling watercourse, often negotiating moss-covered stepping stones. Even at the best of times it's muddy, though, as sunlight barely filters through. The upside is the presence of delightful, rare, prehistoric-looking salamanders. Expect to have to clamber over rotting trees and fallen rocks.

At least an hour is spent in this jungle before the sky reappears for good, and the E5 enters an idyllic valley overflowing with olives, grapes and persimmons. Keep R at the road junction for the final 15min through to the diminutive central square of

2hr 30min – Avesa (97m), where a signboard declares 'Qui termina il Sentiero Europeo E5' ('the European Pathway E5 ends here'). Refreshments galore, groceries, frequent buses to Verona (buy tickets beforehand at the newsagent).

An enjoyable 20min bus trip will see you in beautiful Verona (59m), set on the Adige river and home to the most famous star-crossed lovers in the world, Romeo and Juliet. There is also an excellent natural history museum, with superb fossils of the likes of crocodiles and palm trees, from the prehistoric time when the surrounding mountains were, surprisingly, tropical tidal flats. On the other hand, opera lovers will appreciate a night out in summer at the spectacular Roman Arena. ① (39) 045/8068680. Plenty of accommodation, such as Hotel Torcolo ☎ (39) 045/8007512 **www.hoteltorcolo.it**, and the city's youth hostel ☎ (39) 045/590360 **www.ostellionline.org** a short bus ride out of town.

APPENDIX 1
Tourist Information

Each country has an official tourist information website, packed with useful information and links.

Austria	**www.austria.info**
Germany	**www.germany-tourism.de**
Italy	**www.enit.it**
Switzerland	**www.myswitzerland.com**

Tourist offices that are useful en route are listed here in alphabetical order with their web sites. They also appear in the route description at the relevant point, denoted by ①.

Arbon	☎ (41) 071/4401380	**www.infocenter-arbon.ch**
Bozen/Bolzano	☎ (39) 0471/307000	**www.bolzano-bozen.it**
Bregenz	☎ (43) 05574/425250	**www.vorarlberg-tourism.at**
Carbonare di Folgaria	☎ (39) 0464/765377	**www.montagnaconamore.it**
Cembra	☎ (39) 0461/683110	**www.aptpinecembra.it**
Deutschnofen/ Nova Ponente	☎ (39) 0471/610310	**www.rosengarten-latemar.com**
Folgaria	☎ (39) 0464/721133	**www.montagnaconamore.it**
Hittisau	☎ (43) 05513/6209	**www.hittisau.at**
Holzgau	☎ (43) 05633/5356	**www.lechtal.at**
Jenesien/San Genesio	☎ (39) 0471/354196	**www.jenesien.net**
Konstanz	☎ (49) 07531/133030	**www.konstanz.de/tourismus**
Kreuzlingen	☎ (41) 0171/6723840	**www.kreuzlingen.to**
Levico Terme	☎ (39) 0461/706101	**www.valsugana.info**
Lingenau	☎ (43) 05513/6321	
Luserna	☎ (39) 0464/789638	**www.lusern.it**
Meran/Merano	☎ (39) 0473/272000	**www.meraninfo.it**
Moos Passeier/ Moso in Passiria	☎ (39) 0473/643558	**www.hinterpasseier.com**
Oberstdorf	☎ (49) 0833/700217	**www.oberstdorf.de**
Radein/Redagno	☎ (39) 0471/886800	**www.aldein-radein.it**
Romanshorn	☎ (41) 071/4633232	**www.romanshorn.ch/tourismus**

Rorschach	☎ (41) 071/8417034	**www.tourist-rorschach.ch**
Rovereto	☎ (39) 0464/430363	**www.aptrovereto.it**
Sölden	☎ (43) 05254/510	**www.soelden.com**
Sonthofen	☎ (49) 08321/615291	**www.sonthofen.de/tourismus**
St. Leonhard in Passeier/San Leonardo		
in Passiria	☎ (39) 0473/656188	**www.passeiertal.org**
Truden/Trodena	☎ (39) 0471/869078	**www.trudnerhorn.com**
Valle dei		
Mocheni	☎ (39) 0461/551440	**www.valledeimocheni.it**
Verona	☎ (39) 045/8068680	**www.tourism.verona.it**
Wenns	☎ (43) 05414/86999	**www.pitztal.com**
Zams	☎ (43) 05442/63395	**www.tirolwest.at**

APPENDIX 2
German–English Glossary

German	English	German	English
Ach, Aache	stream, watercourse	*Bühel, Bühl*	hill
Alm	Alpine summer farm, pasture	*Burg*	castle
Alp, Alpe	Alpine pasture	*Dorf*	village
Altstadt	old town centre	*Fahrkarte*	ticket
Auskunft	information	*Fahrplan*	timetable
Aussicht	panorama	*Ferner*	glacier
Autobahn	motorway	*frei/besetzt*	free/occupied
Bach	stream	*Fußgänger*	
Bad	bath	*gestattet*	pedestrians permitted
Bahnhof	railway station	*Fußweg*	footpath
Bäckerei	bakery	*Garni*	bed and breakfast
Berg	mountain	*Gasthaus*	inn, restaurant, hotel
Berghütte	walkers' hut	*Gefahr!*	danger!
Bergstation/		*Geldautomat*	ATM
Talstation	upper station/lower station	*Gletscher*	glacier
	(for cable-car)	*Graben*	ditch, depression
Boden	ground, land	*Grat*	crest
Brücke	bridge	*Grenze*	frontier, border
Brunnen	spring, fountain	*Hafen*	port

German	English
Haltstelle	bus stop
Haus	house
Höhe	upland
Hof	inn, farm, courtyard
Horn	point
Hütte	hut, refuge
Jausenstation	refreshments
Joch	mountain pass, saddle
Jugendherberge	youth hostel
Kamm	ridge
Kapelle	chapel
kein Trinkwasser	undrinkable water
Kirche	church
Klamm	gorge
Kofel, Kopf	peak
Krankenhaus	hospital
Lebensmittel	groceries
Loch	hole
Materialseilbahn	goods lift in mountains
Moos	marsh
Mühl	mill
Nock	peak, point
Ortsmitte	town centre
Parkplatz	car park
Pichl	hillock
Quelle	spring (water)
Radweg	bicycle track
Rundwanderweg	circular pathway

German	English
Säge	sawmill
Sattel	saddle, pass
Scharte	mountain pass, saddle
Schloss	castle
Schlucht	canyon, gorge
See	lake
Seilbahn	cable-car
Spitze	peak
Steig	pathway
Stein	stone
Strasse	street, road
Stunde (abbreviated as *Std*)	hour
Tal	valley
Tobel	ravine
Turm	tower
Wald	wood
Wand	wall, rock point
Wanderweg	pathway, footpath
Wanderer	walker
Wanderkarte	walking map
Wasserfall	waterfall
Weg	way, pathway
Wirtshaus	inn
Wiese	meadow
Zimmer	rooms to rent
Zoll	customs point
Zug	train

APPENDIX 3
Italian–English Glossary

Italian	English
acqua (non) potabile	water (not) suitable for drinking

Italian	English
acqua sorgiva	spring water
affittacamera	bed and breakfast

Italian	English
albergo	hotel
alimentari	groceries
alpe	high-altitude summer pasture, farm
altopiano/altipiano	plateau
autostrada	motorway
bagni, terme	baths, spa
bivacco	unmanned hut for mountaineers
bocca, bocchetta	mountain pass, saddle
borgata	hamlet
bosco	wood
cabinovia	gondola car lift
canalone	gully
capanna	hut
carta dei sentieri,	
carta escursionistica	walking map
casa	house
cascata	waterfall
caserma	military barracks
castello	castle
cava	quarry
chiesa	church
cima	peak
colle	mountain pass
comune	local council district
conca	valley basin, cirque
costa, cresta	ridge
diga	dam
divieto di caccia	no hunting
fermata dell'autobus	bus stop
fonte, sorgente	spring, fountain
frazione	hamlet
funivia	cable-car
galleria	tunnel
gestore	guardian, custodian
giro	tour, circuit
gola	gorge
grotta	cave
inferiore	lower
ingresso	entrance

Italian	English
lago	lake
lavatoio	washing trough
malga	Alpine dairy farm
mulattiera	mule track
municipio	town hall
osteria	tavern, wine bar, simple restaurant
panificio	bakery
passerella	simple bridge
passo	mountain pass
pasticceria	cake shop
pian, piano	flat, plain, basin
ponte	bridge
progno	watercourse
punta	point, summit
ricovero invernale	winter shelter adjoining a refuge
rifugio	mountain hut, usually manned in summer
riserva di caccia	hunting reserve
ristoro	snack bar, place to eat
seggiovia	chair lift
sella	saddle, mountain pass
sentiero	path
sorgente	source of river, spring
stazione ferroviaria	railway station
strada	road
superiore	upper
teleferica	mechanised goods cableway
torrente	mountain stream
trattoria	rustic restaurant
uscita	exit
vaio	valley-like depression, bed of watercourse
valle, vallone	valley
vendita formaggi	cheese on sale

LISTING OF CICERONE GUIDES

BACKPACKING
The End to End Trail
Three Peaks, Ten Tors
Backpacker's Britain Vol 1 – Northern England
Backpacker's Britain Vol 2 – Wales
Backpacker's Britain Vol 3 – Northern Scotland
The Book of the Bivvy

NORTHERN ENGLAND LONG-DISTANCE TRAILS
The Dales Way
The Reiver's Way
The Alternative Coast to Coast
A Northern Coast to Coast Walk
The Pennine Way
Hadrian's Wall Path
The Teesdale Way

FOR COLLECTORS OF SUMMITS
The Relative Hills of Britain
Mts England & Wales Vol 2 – England
Mts England & Wales Vol 1 – Wales

BRITISH CYCLE GUIDES
The Cumbria Cycle Way
Lands End to John O'Groats – Cycle Guide
Rural Rides No.1 – West Surrey
Rural Rides No.2 – East Surrey
South Lakeland Cycle Rides
Border Country Cycle Routes
Lancashire Cycle Way

CANOE GUIDES
Canoeist's Guide to the North-East

LAKE DISTRICT AND MORECAMBE BAY
Coniston Copper Mines
Scrambles in the Lake District (North)
Scrambles in the Lake District (South)
Walks in Silverdale and Arnside AONB
Short Walks in Lakeland 1 – South
Short Walks in Lakeland 2 – North
Short Walks in Lakeland 3 – West
The Tarns of Lakeland Vol 1 – West
The Tarns of Lakeland Vol 2 – East
The Cumbria Way & Allerdale Ramble
Lake District Winter Climbs
Roads and Tracks of the Lake District
The Lake District Angler's Guide
Rocky Rambler's Wild Walks
An Atlas of the English Lakes
Tour of the Lake District
The Cumbria Coastal Way

NORTH-WEST ENGLAND
Walker's Guide to the Lancaster Canal
Family Walks in the Forest Of Bowland
Walks in Ribble Country
Historic Walks in Cheshire
Walking in Lancashire

Walks in Lancashire Witch Country
The Ribble Way

THE ISLE OF MAN
Walking on the Isle of Man
The Isle of Man Coastal Path

PENNINES AND NORTH-EAST ENGLAND
Walks in the Yorkshire Dales
Walks on the North York Moors, books 1 and 2
Walking in the South Pennines
Walking in the North Pennines
Walking in the Wolds
Waterfall Walks – Teesdale and High Pennines
Walking in County Durham
Yorkshire Dales Angler's Guide
Walks in Dales Country
Historic Walks in North Yorkshire
South Pennine Walks
Walking in Northumberland
Cleveland Way and Yorkshire Wolds Way
The North York Moors

DERBYSHIRE, PEAK DISTRICT, EAST MIDLANDS
High Peak Walks
White Peak Walks Northern Dales
White Peak Walks Southern Dales
Star Family Walks Peak District & South Yorkshire
Walking In Peakland
Historic Walks in Derbyshire

WALES AND WELSH BORDERS
Ascent of Snowdon
Welsh Winter Climbs
Hillwalking in Wales – Vol 1
Hillwalking in Wales – Vol 2
Scrambles in Snowdonia
Hillwalking in Snowdonia
The Ridges of Snowdonia
Hereford & the Wye Valley
Walking Offa's Dyke Path
Lleyn Peninsula Coastal Path
Anglesey Coast Walks
The Shropshire Way
Spirit Paths of Wales
Glyndwr's Way
The Pembrokeshire Coastal Path
Walking in Pembrokeshire
The Shropshire Hills – A Walker's Guide

MIDLANDS
The Cotswold Way
The Grand Union Canal Walk
Walking in Warwickshire
Walking in Worcestershire
Walking in Staffordshire
Heart of England Walks

SOUTHERN ENGLAND
Exmoor & the Quantocks
Walking in the Chilterns

Walking in Kent
Two Moors Way
Walking in Dorset
A Walker's Guide to the Isle of Wight
Walking in Somerset
The Thames Path
Channel Island Walks
Walking in Buckinghamshire
The Isles of Scilly
Walking in Hampshire
Walking in Bedfordshire
The Lea Valley Walk
Walking in Berkshire
The Definitive Guide to Walking in London
The Greater Ridgeway
Walking on Dartmoor
The South West Coast Path
Walking in Sussex
The North Downs Way
The South Downs Way

SCOTLAND
Scottish Glens 1 – Cairngorm Glens
Scottish Glens 2 – Atholl Glens
Scottish Glens 3 – Glens of Rannoch
Scottish Glens 4 – Glens of Trossach
Scottish Glens 5 – Glens of Argyll
Scottish Glens 6 – The Great Glen
Scottish Glens 7 – The Angus Glens
Scottish Glens 8 – Knoydart to Morvern
Scottish Glens 9 – The Glens of Ross-shire
The Island of Rhum
Torridon – A Walker's Guide
Walking the Galloway Hills
Border Pubs & Inns – A Walkers' Guide
Scrambles in Lochaber
Walking in the Hebrides
Central Highlands: 6 Long Distance Walks
Walking in the Isle of Arran
Walking in the Lowther Hills
North to the Cape
The Border Country – A Walker's Guide
Winter Climbs – Cairngorms
The Speyside Way
Winter Climbs – Ben Nevis & Glencoe
The Isle of Skye, A Walker's Guide
The West Highland Way
Scotland's Far North
Walking the Munros Vol 1 – Southern, Central
Walking the Munros Vol 2 – Northern & Cairngorms
Scotland's Far West
Walking in the Cairngorms
Walking in the Ochils, Campsie Fells and Lomond Hills
Scotland's Mountain Ridges

The Great Glen Way
The Pentland Hills: A Walker's Guide
The Southern Upland Way

IRELAND
The Mountains of Ireland
Irish Coastal Walks
The Irish Coast to Coast

INTERNATIONAL CYCLE GUIDES
The Way of St James – Le Puy to
    Santiago cyclist's guide
The Danube Cycle Way
Cycle Tours in Spain
Cycling the River Loire – The Way
    of St Martin
Cycle Touring in France
Cycling in the French Alps

WALKING AND TREKKING
IN THE ALPS
Tour of Monte Rosa
Walking in the Alps (all Alpine areas)
100 Hut Walks in the Alps
Chamonix to Zermatt
Tour of Mont Blanc
Alpine Ski Mountaineering
    Vol 1 Western Alps
Alpine Ski Mountaineering
    Vol 2 Eastern Alps
Snowshoeing: Techniques and Routes
    in the Western Alps
Alpine Points of View
Tour of the Matterhorn
Across the Eastern Alps: E5

FRANCE, BELGIUM AND
LUXEMBOURG
RLS (Robert Louis Stevenson) Trail
Walks in Volcano Country
French Rock
Walking the French Gorges
Rock Climbs Belgium & Luxembourg
Tour of the Oisans: GR54
Walking in the Tarentaise and
    Beaufortain Alps
Walking in the Haute Savoie, vol. 1
Walking in the Haute Savoie, vol. 2
Tour of the Vanoise
GR20 Corsica – The High Level Route
The Ecrins National Park
Walking the French Alps: GR5
Walking in the Cevennes
Vanoise Ski Touring
Walking in Provence
Walking on Corsica
Mont Blanc Walks
Walking in the Cathar region
    of south west France
Walking in the Dordogne
Trekking in the Vosges and Jura
The Cathar Way

PYRENEES AND FRANCE / SPAIN
Rock Climbs in the Pyrenees
Walks & Climbs in the Pyrenees
The GR10 Trail: Through the
    French Pyrenees
The Way of St James –
    Le Puy to the Pyrenees
The Way of St James –

Pyrenees-Santiago-Finisterre
Through the Spanish Pyrenees GR11
The Pyrenees – World's Mountain
    Range Guide
The Pyrenean Haute Route
The Mountains of Andorra

SPAIN AND PORTUGAL
Picos de Europa – Walks & Climbs
The Mountains of Central Spain
Walking in Mallorca
Costa Blanca Walks Vol 1
Costa Blanca Walks Vol 2
Walking in Madeira
Via de la Plata (Seville To Santiago)
Walking in the Cordillera Cantabrica
Walking in the Canary Islands 1 West
Walking in the Canary Islands 2 East
Walking in the Sierra Nevada
Walking in the Algarve

SWITZERLAND
Walking in Ticino, Switzerland
Central Switzerland –
    A Walker's Guide
The Bernese Alps
Walking in the Valais
Alpine Pass Route
Walks in the Engadine, Switzerland
Tour of the Jungfrau Region

GERMANY AND AUSTRIA
Klettersteig Scrambles in
    Northern Limestone Alps
King Ludwig Way
Walking in the Salzkammergut
Walking in the Harz Mountains
Germany's Romantic Road
Mountain Walking in Austria
Walking the River Rhine Trail
Trekking in the Stubai Alps
Trekking in the Zillertal Alps

SCANDINAVIA
Walking In Norway
The Pilgrim Road to Nidaros
    (St Olav's Way)

EASTERN EUROPE
The High Tatras
The Mountains of Romania
Walking in Hungary

CROATIA AND SLOVENIA
Walks in the Julian Alps
Walking in Croatia

ITALY
Italian Rock
Walking in the Central Italian Alps
Central Apennines of Italy
Walking in Italy's Gran Paradiso
Long Distance Walks in Italy's Gran
    Paradiso
Walking in Sicily
Shorter Walks in the Dolomites
Treks in the Dolomites
Via Ferratas of the Italian
    Dolomites Vol 1
Via Ferratas of the Italian
    Dolomites Vol 2
Walking in the Dolomites

Walking in Tuscany
Trekking in the Apennines
Through the Italian Alps: the GTA

OTHER MEDITERRANEAN
COUNTRIES
The Mountains of Greece
Climbs & Treks in the Ala Dag
    (Turkey)
The Mountains of Turkey
Treks & Climbs Wadi Rum, Jordan
Jordan – Walks, Treks, Caves etc.
Crete – The White Mountains
Walking in Western Crete
Walking in Malta

AFRICA
Climbing in the Moroccan Anti-Atlas
Trekking in the Atlas Mountains
Kilimanjaro

NORTH AMERICA
The Grand Canyon &
    American South West
Walking in British Columbia
The John Muir Trail

SOUTH AMERICA
Aconcagua

HIMALAYAS – NEPAL, INDIA
Langtang, Gosainkund &
    Helambu: A Trekkers' Guide
Garhwal & Kumaon –
    A Trekkers' Guide
Kangchenjunga – A Trekkers' Guide
Manaslu – A Trekkers' Guide
Everest – A Trekkers' Guide
Annapurna – A Trekker's Guide
Bhutan – A Trekker's Guide

TECHNIQUES AND EDUCATION
The Adventure Alternative
Rope Techniques
Snow & Ice Techniques
Mountain Weather
Beyond Adventure
The Hillwalker's Manual
Outdoor Photography
The Hillwalker's Guide to
    Mountaineering
Map and Compass

MINI GUIDES
Avalanche!
Snow
Pocket First Aid and Wilderness
    Medicine
Mountain Navigation

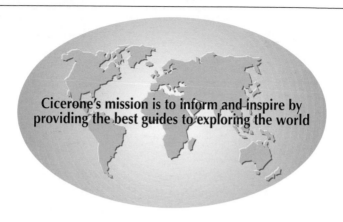

Cicerone's mission is to inform and inspire by
providing the best guides to exploring the world

Since its foundation over 30 years ago, Cicerone has specialised in publishing guidebooks and has built a reputation for quality and reliability. It now publishes nearly 300 guides to the major destinations for outdoor enthusiasts, including Europe, UK and the rest of the world.

Written by leading and committed specialists, Cicerone guides are recognised as the most authoritative. They are full of information, maps and illustrations so that the user can plan and complete a successful and safe trip or expedition – be it a long face climb, a walk over Lakeland fells, an alpine traverse, a Himalayan trek or a ramble in the countryside.

With a thorough introduction to assist planning, clear diagrams, maps and colour photographs to illustrate the terrain and route, and accurate and detailed text, Cicerone guides are designed for ease of use and access to the information.

If the facts on the ground change, or there is any aspect of a guide that you think we can improve, we are always delighted to hear from you.

Cicerone Press
2 Police Square Milnthorpe Cumbria LA7 7PY
Tel:01539 562 069   Fax:01539 563 417
e-mail:info@cicerone.co.uk   web:www.cicerone.co.uk

CICERONE